Racism

Editor: Tracy Biram

Volume 376

independence
educational publishers

First published by Independence Educational Publishers

The Studio, High Green

Great Shelford

Cambridge CB22 5EG

England

© Independence 2020

Copyright

Photocopy licence

ISBN-13: 978 1 86168 833 0

Printed in Great Britain

Zenith Print Group

Contents

Introduction

Racism is Volume 376 in the **issues** series. The aim of the series is to offer current, diverse information about important issues in our world, from a UK perspective.

ABOUT RACISM

Racism is more than name-calling, it is all around us. From microaggressions to violent hate crimes, incidents of racial prejudice and ethnic discrimination are never far from headlines. This book explores the issue of racism in the UK today. It looks at the recent resurgence of the Black Lives Matter movement, Islamophobia, antisemitism and other communites affected by discrimination. It also looks at ways to tackle the problem.

OUR SOURCES

Titles in the **issues** series are designed to function as educational resource books, providing a balanced overview of a specific subject.

The information in our books is comprised of facts, articles and opinions from many different sources, including:

♦ Newspaper reports and opinion pieces

♦ Website factsheets

♦ Magazine and journal articles

♦ Statistics and surveys

♦ Government reports

♦ Literature from special interest groups.

A NOTE ON CRITICAL EVALUATION

Because the information reprinted here is from a number of different sources, readers should bear in mind the origin of the text and whether the source is likely to have a particular bias when presenting information (or when conducting their research). It is hoped that, as you read about the many aspects of the issues explored in this book, you will critically evaluate the information presented.

It is important that you decide whether you are being presented with facts or opinions. Does the writer give a biased or unbiased report? If an opinion is being expressed, do you agree with the writer? Is there potential bias to the 'facts' or statistics behind an article?

ASSIGNMENTS

In the back of this book, you will find a selection of assignments designed to help you engage with the articles you have been reading and to explore your own opinions. Some tasks will take longer than others and there is a mixture of design, writing and research-based activities that you can complete alone or in a group.

FURTHER RESEARCH

At the end of each article we have listed its source and a website that you can visit if you would like to conduct your own research. Please remember to critically evaluate any sources that you consult and consider whether the information you are viewing is accurate and unbiased.

Useful Websites

www.annefrank.org

www.childline.org.uk

www.cipd.co.uk

www.creativereview.co.uk

www.equalityhumanrights.com

www.historicengland.org.uk

www.independent.co.uk

wtww.inews.co.uk

www.kickitout.org

www.kingsfund..org.uk

www.metro.co.uk

www.prospectmagazine.co.uk

www.schoolsweek.co.uk

www.stophateuk.org

www.telegraph.co.uk

www.theconversation.com

www.theguardian.com

www.yougov.co.uk

The truth about racism in the UK

In December, grime artist Stormzy caused a media frenzy by pointing out the UK's racism. Here, Jude Yawson, co-author with Stormzy on his book *Rise Up*, calls out the hypocrisy that exists in UK media and explains why we urgently need wider representation in our culture.

By Jude Yawson

To exist as a historically conscious black or Asian person in Britain is to exist knowing that a majority of your white counterparts do not acknowledge your history. They have not been forced to adopt centuries of trauma, or been subjected to the racialised perceptions created over that time. They have not originated from mother countries gradually drying from the imperialism they were soaked in, and do not have to live in recognition of slavery and colonialism and the impact these have had on their countries and people.

They will never walk around a university campus surrounded by artefacts stolen from other countries, or see the colonialists who ravaged their mother countries celebrated as heroic figures. Nor will they see them hosted in museums – establishments that fight to keep artefacts for tourism's sake. Or witness their own people depicted in galleries as slaves, without any recognisable history.

They do not have to come to terms with being 'otherised' in almost every way while watching the mainstay of society have a freedom of history that they don't. They can see their history as subjectively as they like – as entertainment or, in the case of memorials or the beloved poppy, a meaningful necessity to recall. History written and projected by the victorious, that has no enticement for the other as it is meaningless to their immediate lives. Hence, I question how truly 'great' Britain is, and how great does Britain want the livelihoods and perceptions of all its people to be? Undoing the social and spiritual disease that is racism is a necessity.

'A plethora of black and Asian Brits, who mostly have experienced racism at a micro, macro, and systematic level, exist and combat it.'

In recent months, the media has leveraged a wayward discussion on whether this country is racist. There is a lack of interconnectivity in this. For instance, reports of hate crime have increased steadily over the past several years, increasing significantly after Brexit. And temporary exclusions in primary school for incidents of racism have gone up, which makes me wonder about the link between the xenophobic tone of the Brexit campaign and young Brits' growing perceptions of people.

There are examples everywhere. Meghan Markle and her marriage to Prince Harry, their gross treatment within the media reeking of racism after her African American heritage was widely acknowledged. The comparison of their newborn to a monkey by the popular radio show host and DJ Danny Baker. Increasing incidents of racism in football – Raheem Sterling and others being subjected to racist chants.

And then there's the reaction to Stormzy saying the UK is racist, '100%', in terms of its institutional and systematic history. His comment was misrepresented by media – suggesting he'd said that Britain is 100% racist, as in entirely racist. His character was attacked and he was subjected to racist and derogatory comments simply for speaking out. He was then accused of being too affluent to experience racism, despite having had his door kicked in by police who were called to his house by neighbours suspicious that a black man had let himself into a lovely home, in a wealthy Chelsea neighbourhood.

'There is a catalogue of racist events that are widely acknowledged in our communities but rarely acknowledged by white people.'

A plethora of black and Asian Brits, who mostly have experienced racism at a micro, macro, and systematic level, exist and combat it every day to different degrees. But on the largest platforms – *Good Morning Britain*, Sky, *Question Time* – such experiences are dismissed, sometimes as 'pandering to wokeness' as opposed to what they truly are: a soulful endeavour to alleviate us from this entrenched position. While posing as a debate and offering people who do not suffer from racism a perspective, such platforms are doing a grave disservice to the honest work of the well-studied and concerned people who can communicate such experiences.

Good Morning Britain host Piers Morgan recently had what many in media referred to as a 'fiery debate' with British writer and broadcaster Afua Hirsch live on TV. He did not afford her any time to articulate herself, her words misconstrued and attacked, her points belittled with counter arguments that strayed from the issue. In the same breath, Morgan defended Danny Baker. Racism itself as a phenomenon becomes a blurred line.

On the TV show *This Morning*, Dr Shola Mos-Shogbamimu described white privilege, where incidents such as Baker's racist tweet and the microaggressions mounted against Meghan Markle can be dismissed as playful ignorance and not denoted as racism. She argued that it is not the job of black people or minorities to teach white people about racism, they must endeavour to learn about it themselves. Presenter Phillip Schofield asked, 'What examples do you have?' to which Mos-Shogbamimu pointed out that his question is precisely the issue, and asked where has he been in the past two years.

There is a catalogue of racist events that are widely acknowledged in our communities but rarely acknowledged by white people because they do not have to live with the realisation or memory of it. It has no bearing on their lives.

Racism becomes a stance, often described as the 'race card', which implies people have been allowed to see such a conversation as debatable rather than wholly misunderstood. This is maintained by our media. In an article for *The Guardian*, Hirsch noted how slow the acknowledgement of racism is in Britain. She argued that the notion of the 'race card' is being used to silence people from speaking out on racial matters. There is a difficulty in decolonising and proposing anti-racist rhetoric even at a school level. Hirsch referred to the University of Sheffield, which is paying 20 race equality champions to tackle racism on campus. Their work includes tackling derogatory statements, such as 'you are pretty for a black girl' or 'you are playing the race card'. As Hirsch states, these magical cards don't work.

Yet microaggressions are one feat of many that coincide with racism. If this well educated, intelligent and good intentioned woman can be vilified – who can't be? It becomes a constant battle, a fight into which we all can be involuntarily dragged, even if we jeopardise our positions for doing so – socially or financially.

'Racism becomes a stance, often described as the "race card", which implies people have been allowed to see such a conversation as debatable.'

DJ Dotty recently took such a risk, calling out her employer on her BBC 1Xtra Breakfast radio show for showing clips of LeBron James when reporting on the untimely passing of Kobe Bryant in a BBC News report. The two basketball players look entirely different – the only similarity is they both played for the Lakers. She described this as unforgivable and placed her company in the Trash Bag – a feature of her show where she highlights something that needs to be addressed. Dotty made the point that the BBC would never have confused Messi with Ronaldo, Nadal with Federer, and that not all black people look the same. The lackadaisical incompetence of the BBC, with the correct information available in 0.2 seconds of research (James' name on the back of his shirt was clearly legible in the footage), makes you wonder what taxpayers are paying for.

Self-made writers and artists are using social media and their wider media platforms to speak out against the racism that impacts all corners of society. Raheem Sterling has used his platform to point toward racism on and off the pitch, including calling out biased media headlines. Writers like Musa Okwonga have spoken out on racism within football. Stormzy has used his platform to shed light and respond to the racism exemplified in the media against him and others. Rapper Dave's song *Black* accumulates facets of a young black and powerful livelihood. Writers like Chanté Joseph write on racism within politics and television.

But not only racism, also perspectives of black Britishness – like Aniefiok Ekpoudom shedding light on the brilliance of artists such as J Hus and why he is so important to young, up-and-coming black Brits. Rapman, and his short film *Shiro's Story* and feature-length movie *Blue Story* depicting overshadowed livelihoods. Ciaran Thappar and his articles on Drill music as an entity, providing nuance on topics the mainstream media refuse to tackle, as well as writing on experiences to do with racism from the British Asian community.

'There is a grave and systematic error that pits people against each other, which has become the mainstay of the country.'

These are all self-made individuals who recognise and understand a greater cause in depicting things surrounding race differently. Nevertheless, like Mos-Shogbamimu said, it's not on us individually to explain racism – others must endeavour to unlearn.

There is a grave and systematic error that pits people against each other, which has become the mainstay of the country. If we want to reach a state of equality, the experiences of black and ethnic minorities must be recognised alongside wider Britishness. Whether it's politically, or in the media, or in social media and its algorithms, creating our echo chambers of people – this society as a whole needs to do better.

11 March 2020

Jude Yawson is a writer based in London. He co-authored Rise Up: The #Merky Story So Far with Stormzy, the first book to be released under the Penguin Random House Imprint Merky Books; @judeblay

Race discrimination

What is race discrimination?

This is when you are treated differently because of your race in one of the situations covered by the Equality Act.

The treatment could be a one-off action or as a result of a rule or policy based on race. It doesn't have to be intentional to be unlawful.

There are some circumstances when being treated differently due to race is lawful, explained below.

What the Equality Act says about race discrimination

The Equality Act 2010 says you must not be discriminated against because of your race.

In the Equality Act, race can mean your colour, or your nationality (including your citizenship). It can also mean your ethnic or national origins, which may not be the same as your current nationality. For example, you may have Chinese national origins and be living in Britain with a British passport.

Race also covers ethnic and racial groups. This means a group of people who all share the same protected characteristic of ethnicity or race.

A racial group can be made up of two or more distinct racial groups, for example black Britons, British Asians, British Sikhs, British Jews, Romany Gypsies and Irish Travellers.

You may be discriminated against because of one or more aspects of your race, for example people born in Britain to Jamaican parents could be discriminated against because they are British citizens, or because of their Jamaican national origins.

Different types of race discrimination

There are four main types of race discrimination

Direct discrimination

This happens when someone treats you worse than another person in a similar situation because of your race. For example:

♦ if a letting agency would not let a flat to you because of your race, this would be direct race discrimination

Indirect discrimination

This happens when an organisation has a particular policy or way of working that puts people of your racial group at a disadvantage. For example:

a hairdresser refuses to employ stylists that cover their own hair, this would put any Muslim women or Sikh men who cover their hair at a disadvantage when applying for a position as a stylist

Sometimes indirect race discrimination can be permitted if the organisation or employer is able to show to show that there is a good reason for the discrimination. This is known as objective justification. For example:

♦ a Somalian asylum seeker tries to open a bank account but the bank states that in order to be eligible you need to have been resident in the UK for 12 months and have a permanent address. The Somalian man is not able to open a bank account. The bank would need to prove that its policy was necessary for business reasons (such as to prevent fraud) and that there was no practical alternative

Harrassment

Harassment occurs when someone makes you feel humiliated, offended or degraded. For example:

♦ a young British Asian man at work keeps being called a racist name by colleagues. His colleagues say it is just banter, but the employee is insulted and offended by it

Harassment can never be justified. However, if an organisation or employer can show it did everything it could to prevent people who work for it from behaving like that, you will not be able to make a claim for harassment against it, although you could make a claim against the harasser.

Victimisation

This is when you are treated badly because you have made a complaint of race related discrimination under the Equality Act. It can also occur if you are supporting someone who has made a complaint of race related discrimination. For example:

♦ the young man in the example above wants to make a formal complaint about his treatment. His manager threatens to sack him unless he drops the complaint

Circumstances when being treated differently due to race is lawful

A difference in treatment may be lawful in employment situations if:

♦ belonging to a particular race is essential for the job. This is called an occupational requirement. For example, an organisation wants to recruit a support worker for a domestic violence advice service for South Asian women. The organisation can say that it only wants to employ someone with South Asian origins

♦ an organisation is taking positive action to encourage or develop people in a racial group that is under-represented or disadvantaged in a role or activity. For example, a broadcaster gets hardly any applicants for its graduate recruitment programme from Black Caribbean candidates. It sets up a work experience and mentoring programme for Black Caribbean students to encourage them into the industry

19 February 2020

84% of BAME Britons think the UK is still very or somewhat racist

With Black Lives Matter protests dominating headlines, YouGov research reveals that Black, Asian and minority ethnic adults in Britain today believe racism has not reduced in the last three decades.

By Tanya Abraham, Associate Director of Political and Social Research

YouGov interviewed over 1,200 BAME Britons, including people from Black, Asian, Mixed and other non-White backgrounds, about issues of race today and in the past. Worrying results show that virtually identical numbers of people believe racism exists in the country today (84%) as believe it existed 30 years ago (86%). Not only does this figure show that the issue is a problem in the eyes of an overwhelming number of Britons from ethnic minorities, but also that it does not seem to be reducing over time.

However, there is a noticeable difference in severity; seven in ten (68%) think racism was present to 'a great deal' in UK society 30 years ago, and this has fallen to 47% today.

This suggests that the type of racism people experience or witness has changed over time.

Among Black Britons the trend is slightly reversed; 91% recognise its overall presence 30 years ago, and 94% continue to identify it in today's society. This is perhaps a temporary rise linked to the current Black Lives Matter protests.

Interestingly, the older a person is, the more likely they are to say that there was a "great deal" of racism 30 years ago. Among those aged 18 to 24 this response was given by 63% of people, and this rises to 67% among 25 to 49 year olds, 73% among 50 to 64-year-olds and 75% of those over 65. This is perhaps indicative of younger Britons underestimating levels of racism, compared to people who actually lived through that time.

Our survey reveals that race has a greater impact than age or gender on how people are perceived and treated. Nearly two in three (64%) said they are treated differently, rising to 79% of Black and 70% of Chinese respondents.

What counts as racist, and how often does it happen? But what exactly do people count as racist? We can compare results from this latest survey to a previous report on a representative sample of Britons of all races, and see where opinion differs.

Most notably, there is a 20-point difference between BAME respondents who think imitating an accent is racist (60%) and the wider population (41%).

How common have experiences of racism been for BAME Britons?

For each of the following examples, please say whether this has or has not ever happened to you? % of 1,270 BAME adults in GB

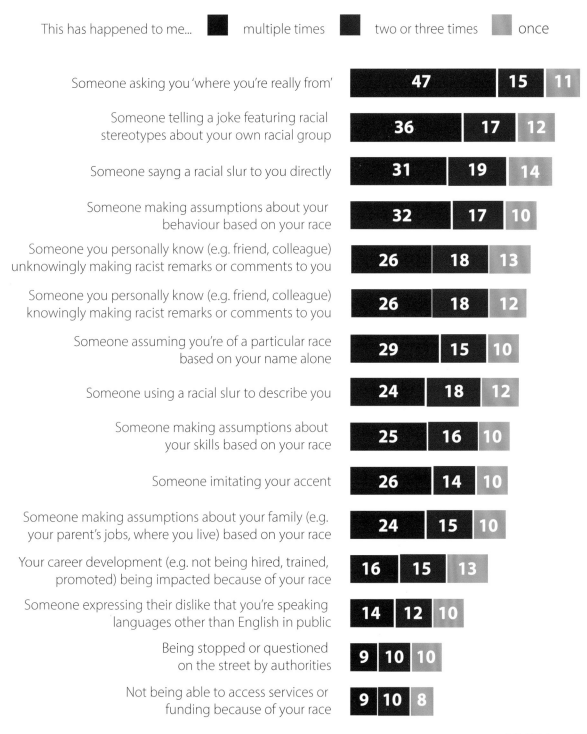

This has happened to me... ■ multiple times ■ two or three times ▨ once

	multiple times	two or three times	once
Someone asking you 'where you're really from'	47	15	11
Someone telling a joke featuring racial stereotypes about your own racial group	36	17	12
Someone sayng a racial slur to you directly	31	19	14
Someone making assumptions about your behaviour based on your race	32	17	10
Someone you personally know (e.g. friend, colleague) unknowingly making racist remarks or comments to you	26	18	13
Someone you personally know (e.g. friend, colleague) knowingly making racist remarks or comments to you	26	18	12
Someone assuming you're of a particular race based on your name alone	29	15	10
Someone using a racial slur to describe you	24	18	12
Someone making assumptions about your skills based on your race	25	16	10
Someone imitating your accent	26	14	10
Someone making assumptions about your family (e.g. your parent's jobs, where you live) based on your race	24	15	10
Your career development (e.g. not being hired, trained, promoted) being impacted because of your race	16	15	13
Someone expressing their dislike that you're speaking languages other than English in public	14	12	10
Being stopped or questioned on the street by authorities	9	10	10
Not being able to access services or funding because of your race	9	10	8

10-17 June 2020

Three in four BAME respondents (75%) think it is racist to dislike people who live in the UK and speak other languages in public, compared to just 58% of Britons in general.

We also asked how many BAME Britons have experienced racism directly: 74% have had someone ask "where you're really from?" and 64% have had a racial slur directed at them. Some 65% have witnessed someone telling a joke featuring a racial stereotype about their own race.

More than half (52%) have been on the receiving end of assumptions based on race, 44% have experienced an impact on their career and 27% say their race impeded access to services or funding. A quarter (29%) have been stopped or questioned on the street by authorities, with 9% citing it has happened multiple times.

When asked about the Metropolitan police today, one in two (50%) think it is institutionally racist; seven in ten Black Britons (69%) share this view compared to around half of other BAME groups.

Black Lives Matter

In the last few weeks protests against the killing of George Floyd whilst under police restraint in the US have spread around the world, including Britain. The majority of BAME respondents polled did not participate in the Black Lives Matter protests (74%) but small groups took part in other ways, for example on social media during the most recent protests (14%).

Despite the low participation, seven in ten (68%) support the demonstrations, with younger people doing so more strongly (76% of those aged 18 to 24) than their older counterparts (66% of those aged over 65). Whilst the majority of all BAME groups back the campaign, support varies from 57% amongst those of Chinese ethnicity to 82% of Black people.

The media coverage has been extensive, but only 51% of respondents thought it has been fair. Some 43% said that the protests had been portrayed as more violent than they actually were. Just over a quarter (29%) think the coverage has been biased against the protests, whilst 31% consider it to have been supportive.

When asked about the impact of the Black Lives Matter protests, 46% think it will have a positive influence overall. A fifth are either ambivalent (20%) or think the protests will have a negative impact (17%).

During the protests, a statue of Edward Colston was thrown into a harbour in Bristol by anti-racism protestors, due to his involvement in the slave trade. Two in three support its removal; of this, 31% approve of how it was removed, whilst 34% think another method would have been preferable.

On a wider level, over half (56%) support the removal of all statues linked to slavery from British towns and cities; just 19% oppose this.

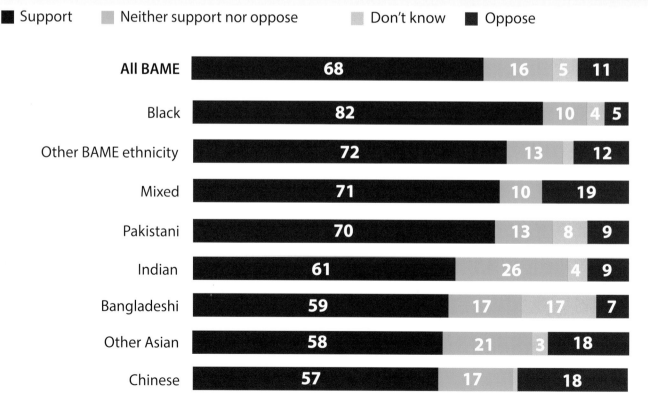

Most BAME Britons support the Black Lives Matter protests, but the extent varies by ethnic group

To what extent do you support or oppose the Black Lives Matter protests?
% of 1,270 BAME adults in GB

■ Support   ■ Neither support nor oppose   ■ Don't know   ■ Oppose

	Support	Neither support nor oppose	Don't know	Oppose
All BAME	68	16	5	11
Black	82	10	4	5
Other BAME ethnicity	72	13		12
Mixed	71	10		19
Pakistani	70	13	8	9
Indian	61	26	4	9
Bangladeshi	59	17	17	7
Other Asian	58	21	3	18
Chinese	57	17		18

10-17 June 2020

Most BAME Britons want to see changes to the school curriculum, with history at the top of the list

% of 1,270 BAME adults in GB

Thinking about British schools today, some people have called for curriculums to reflect more of Britain's colonial past and diversity whilst others have said that this is not required. Which of the following best reflects your view?

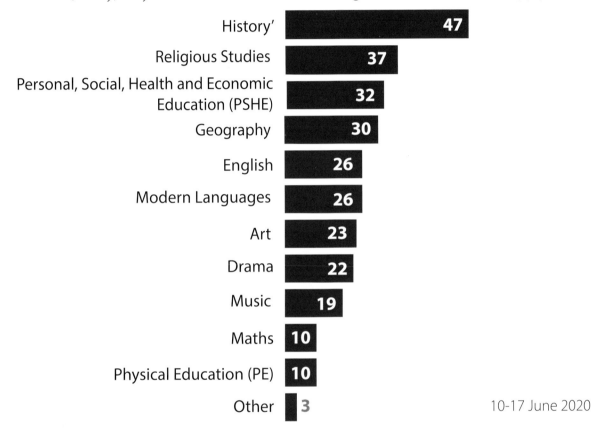

There should not be changes — 15

There should be changes — 69

In which areas, if any, do you think there should be changes? (Please tick all that apply)

History' — 47

Religious Studies — 37

Personal, Social, Health and Economic Education (PSHE) — 32

Geography — 30

English — 26

Modern Languages — 26

Art — 23

Drama — 22

Music — 19

Maths — 10

Physical Education (PE) — 10

Other — 3

10-17 June 2020

Two in five are now educating themselves about race issues

Perhaps as a result of the protests, 43% say they are listening to and reading more about issues related to racism now than before. Half of 18 to 24 year olds (49%) and Black people (48%) share this view.

Over half think it important to have conversations about racism with family (53%) and friends of different race (54%), and there is also evidence of support for changes to the education system. The majority (69%) are in favour of updating the school curriculum to include Britain's colonial past. Just 15% do not think there should be any change.

Of those who support changing the curriculum, nearly nine in ten (87%) think history should be updated. Around half think religious studies (53%) should be adapted, whilst others identify PSHE (47%) and geography (44%).

Fair representation in the workplace and beyond

When it comes to the workplace, just over half of those in employment (56%) consider it a diverse environment, whilst 34% do not. The plurality (46%) are satisfied with their workplace policies, but a quarter remain displeased (27%). On a broader level, and based on their exposure, most think there is unfair representation of ethnic minorities amongst scientists and experts (48%), politicians (55%) and industry or business leaders (56%).

26 June 2020

How racist is Britain today? What the evidence tells us

An article from The Conversation.

By Anthony Heath and Lindsay Richards

THE CONVERSATION

When seeking to get a picture of the inequality and social injustice faced by black and minority ethnic groups in the UK, a good place to start is the government's own figures.

It's starkly evident that major ethnic and racial inequalities persist in employment, housing and the justice system. Black and Muslim minorities have twice the unemployment rate of their white British peers and are twice as likely to live in overcrowded housing. They are also much more likely to be stopped and searched by the police. We could also add to the list the alarming ethnic differences in deaths from COVID-19.

The government's pioneering ethnicity facts and figures website brings together in a single accessible format the hard evidence on ethnic disparities collected by government departments. It is a world-first, established in 2016 by former prime minister Theresa May, who pledged to tackle "burning injustices".

Critics could plausibly argue that disparities of the kind demonstrated by the website do not, in themselves, prove that racism and discrimination are the driving forces behind the inequalities. But, when combined with other direct evidence, it's hard to avoid concluding that they play a role.

There are two main sorts of direct evidence that show racism and racial injustice continue in Britain – surveys about British people's beliefs and field experiments testing whether minorities receive equal treatment in practice.

Racist beliefs

Let's look at racist beliefs first. Through the European Social Survey, we asked a representative sample of the British public two questions on "biological racism" – that is, the belief that there are innate differences between racial or ethnic groups. A belief that innate differences make some groups inherently superior to others is generally taken to be the core idea of racism.

We asked whether interviewees agreed that "some races or ethnic groups are born less intelligent than others" and found that 18% of the British public agreed with the statement. We also asked whether "some races or ethnic groups are born harder working than others", to which a substantially larger percentage – 44% – said yes.

Perhaps the difference between these two percentages is due to political correctness.

The claim that there are innate group differences in intelligence would widely be recognised as a racist statement, whereas innate differences in work ethic may not have the same blatant connotations. But whether we go for the lower or the higher figure, on this evidence a substantial

minority of the British public subscribe to some form of racist belief.

We repeated these questions on biological racism in a more recent (2019) nationally representative online survey. The findings were very similar – 19% agreed that some groups were born less intelligent, and 38% agreed that some groups were born less hard working. We also found that people who subscribed to these racist beliefs were more likely to be opposed to immigration and to express other "nativist" views, such as that one needs to have English ancestry to be truly English.

People who express agreement with these racist statements in an interview may not necessarily act on them in practice. But the finding is in line with minorities' own reports that they experience racial hostility and harassment in their daily lives.

Discriminatory practices

Field experiments can provide more direct evidence about what happens in practice. To investigate discrimination in the job market, researchers typically send matched written applications from fictitious minority and majority-group applicants to advertised vacancies. The applications are identical in all respects and differ only in the names of the applicants, which are selected to be typical British or minority names respectively. Field experiments like these are generally recognised as the "gold standard" for determining whether minorities are at risk of discrimination.

In 2016 and 2017 we carried out a study along these lines. We found that applicants with typically black or Muslim names were much less likely than those with standard British names to receive a positive response from employers. For every ten positive replies that the British applicant (James or Emily) received, a person with a recognisably African (Akintunde or Adeola) or Pakistani name (Tariq or Yasmin) received only six. Minorities with a west European name (Guillaume, for example) were only slightly less likely than the British to obtain a positive callback.

In 2018 The Guardian newspaper conducted a similar field experiment in the private flatshare market. Expressions of interest were sent from "Muhammad" and "David" to almost 1,000 online advertisements for rooms across the UK. The Guardian found that for every 10 positive replies that David received, Muhammad received only eight.

So, government data and field experiments provide pretty conclusive evidence that black and Muslim minorities are at risk of discrimination when looking for a job or home in the UK. They only study the outcome rather than the motivations of the employer or landlord so we can't be sure that they are acting on racist beliefs – but in law it is the outcome that matters. Unequal treatment of applicants is illegal, whatever the motivation.

Rigorous field experiments have not, to our knowledge, been conducted in the criminal justice system but we certainly cannot rule out the possibility that racial stereotyping is behind the disparities in stop and search data recorded by the government.

Racial discrimination may be more widespread than the limited amount of testing carried out has so far proved – just as COVID-19 infections have almost certainly been a great deal more widespread than the testing indicated. We need more testing. But, even more importantly, the testing that has already been carried out indicates a pressing need for real change.

1 July 2020.

The philosophical flaw in saying "All Lives Matter"

Its effect is to stall conversations about anti-Black racism and instead either pretend that all lives do matter, or talk about everybody's lives all at once—whether or not particular groups are subject to particular injustices right now.

By Arianne Shahvisi

One item that survived my recent wardrobe clear-out is a t-shirt emblazoned with the slogan "Refugees are welcome." Taken at face value, it's a lie. In the UK, refugees are decidedly not welcome, and never have been. Asylum seekers' applications are readily rejected, many are detained and deported, and an alarming proportion of refugees are homeless. Yet the statement is meaningful as an expression of hope: I want to live in a world in which refugees are welcome. It's a message of protest, a provocation, an objective.

We often use slogans that aren't strictly true in the hope that stating them publicly prompts a moral conversation which might culminate in their truth. Like "girls can do anything" (in our sexist societies, they clearly can't), or "all love is equal" (again, not without marriage equality, or if homophobia prevails), or the fact that we hold "Pride" marches even though internalised homophobia and transphobia means many people aren't proud. These are rallying calls around which people organise their resistance to injustice. To see their sense, you have to step back and take in their social context: widespread sexism, racism, homophobia, and transphobia.

What do we mean by "Black Lives Matter"?

The Black Lives Matter (BLM) movement grew out of a hashtag that trended in 2013 after George Zimmerman was acquitted of murder, having shot dead a seventeen-year-old Trayvon Martin when he was walking back from a corner shop in Florida, sweets and drink in hand. Seven years later, there has been a new surge of outrage and energy following the recent killings of George Floyd and Breonna Taylor by US police.

The tagline of this growing global movement against anti-Black racism operates similarly to those described above. It expresses mournfulness and anger, but also yearning.

"Black Lives Matter" points to two things:

♦ As far as various major social institutions are concerned—the police, the criminal justice system, medicine—Black lives don't matter as much as other lives.

♦ Black lives should matter as much as other lives.

Taken together, these statements form the basis for challenging anti-Black racism.

The first point is a descriptive statement. It describes the world, and its truth can be verified through data based on observations. In the UK, Black people are five times more likely to die in childbirth than white people, and Black infant mortality is twice as high. Black people are twice as likely as white people to be unemployed, and almost half of Black households live in poverty. Black people are ten times more likely to be stopped and searched than white people, and four times more likely to be arrested. They constitute 3 per cent of the population, but 8 per cent of deaths in police custody. Black lives are deplorably under-valued.

Black is not a scientific term, it's a social one: there is no genetic basis for "Black" as a category, and two Black people chosen at random are likely to have less in common genetically than either has with any given white person. What Black people do have in common is the racism they face, which produces the discrepancies just described.

Turning to the second claim, "Black lives should matter" is what we call a normative statement. It's a moral proclamation, stating it's wrong that Black lives are under-valued. Moral statements cannot be verified by observations; they're based on particular values that must be argued for. (I won't argue that Black lives should matter. If that's not a value you already hold and find obvious, this article is not for you.)

Why not "all lives matter"?

Soon after the inception of the BLM movement, it was itself thwarted by baffling accusations of racism, often accompanied with the rejoinder: "All Lives Matter."

Clearly, as a descriptive statement, this isn't true. Not all lives matter. (Consider the way Black people, other people of colour, refugees, Gypsies and Travellers, and homeless people are treated.) We could instead interpret it as normative statement: all lives should matter. Agreed. Yet context is very important. Note that nobody was saying "All Lives Matter" before 2013. Rather, it's a direct response to BLM, and has no life outside that. And that's a problem, because if BLM is understood as a commitment to urgently tackling the violence and brutality of anti-Black racism, then blurting that "All Lives Matter" is at best tangential, and at worst a malevolent distraction.

Its effect is to stall conversations about anti-Black racism and instead either pretend that all lives do matter, or talk about everybody's lives all at once, whether or not particular groups are subject to particular, potentially fatal injustices right now. This leaves no bandwidth to address the particularly brutal injustices that Black people face. Saying "All Lives Matter" violates the concept of triage in medical ethics, which demands that we address the most troubling or life-endangering issues first.

"All Lives Matter" is therefore an obstacle to tackling anti-Black racism. Sometimes, it's a result of ignorance, a misinterpretation of BLM. More often, it's intentional; a filibuster, bent on derailing anti-racist work.

From bad to worse

Last week, a group of British football fans paid for a banner stating "White Lives Matter" to be flown over a football match in Manchester, right after the players had taken the knee in solidarity with BLM.

Given my arguments for "Black Lives Matter," you might infer that the reasoning carries over to "White Lives Matter" with just one word substituted. Yet white lives are already valued, so what's the fight for? Why fly a banner? White people earn more, are most likely to be employed, and least likely to be arrested. Consider that CVs headed with "white British" names are significantly more likely to get a call-back by UK employers than if they bear names associated with people of colour, even if the text is identical. There's no empirical evidence that white people struggle specifically because they are white. Being white is something that works in a person's favour, even if their life might be hard for other reasons.

And here's the punchline. Many of those defending the football stunt claim to interpret "Black Lives Matter" to mean only black lives matter. They're wrong (see above), but if we follow this logic, it seems reasonable to assume they also think "White Lives Matter" means only white lives matter. That amounts to a statement in support of white supremacy. Anti-Black racism is not a mysterious, hidden phenomenon. Racism does not get more obvious than a person being shot while jogging, or a woman being killed in her bed by police. To send a "White Lives Matter" banner into the sky pushes beyond ignorance towards something far more threatening.

As BLM continues to gain momentum and institutions are compelled to change, we're likely to see more reprisals of this sort. It's a time for hope, but also for vigilance and continual solidarity. Those of us who are allies to this struggle have a duty to make sure the reasoning behind BLM is as clear as possible, so we can push this movement forward through the force of argument as well as the force of justice.

3 July 2020

Can white people experience racism?

In its most simplistic definition, racism is prejudice or discrimination directed at someone of a different race – based on the belief that your own race is superior.

By Natalie Morris

Taking this definition at its word, then, would suggest that it is possible for a person of any race to experience racism if someone treats them badly for this reason – even white people.

But this definition of racism leaves out one crucial element: The power structures that uphold and perpetuate racism.

Racism doesn't exist in a vacuum. It exists within a hierarchical structure with power at its core. Racism only works because one group has power and other groups do not.

And it is white people who – historically, and in the West at least – hold the power when it comes to racial divides, thanks to centuries of Eurocentric beliefs and structures that continue to privilege and centre whiteness.

Think about it in terms of the effects

If an ethnic minority person treats a white person badly because of inherent prejudice against white people, that is wrong and completely unacceptable, but the wider ramifications are likely to be less significant than if it were the other way around.

If a white person treats an ethnic minority badly because of the colour of their skin, not only is it morally wrong, it can also have serious and dangerous implications for the life and prospects of that person.

Prejudice against white people might make individuals feel bad, but prejudice against ethnic minorities can lead to structural, systemic and lasting disadvantages (in education, healthcare, disproportionate policing, career prospects, among other areas), and this is what makes it racism.

White people would only experience racism if the existing power structures enabled prejudice against them to cause this kind of widespread negative impact – as it does for people of colour. But that's not how society currently works.

Can white people experience racial prejudice?

In a word, yes. Stereotypes and negative beliefs about white people are examples of racial prejudice – but not racism.

Which, to be clear, is still wrong. Prejudice directed at any group based on a set of preconceived assumptions is never a good thing, and almost always leads to behaviour that is hurtful and causes harm.

The difference between racial prejudice and racism is the lack of any power structure weighted in favour of a particular race.

'There is no doubt that white people can experience discrimination, harassment and be the victim of prejudice,' explains psychologist and anti-racism scholar Guilaine Kinouani.

'We could even argue in some contexts they can be the victims of racial hatred.

'However, no matter how condemnable these acts or attitudes are, we should be careful, as has been now argued for decades, not to confuse individual acts of prejudice or bigotry with racism, which, as a system, is ubiquitous and determinative of life course, opportunities and experiences.'

Guilaine adds that racism as a system is supported by institutional power and historical myths about the socially constructed inferiority of certain groups; people of colour.

'It is a system which has a history spanning several centuries, a system which has become part of the very fabric of our society and, which ultimately continues to place increased worth on the lives and bodies of white people,' explains Guilaine.

'Fundamentally, without socially sanctioned power, what we're only ever going to be left with is racial bigotry rather than a system of racial oppression.

'This distinction matters, and erasing it is not only intellectually lazy and disingenuous, but it is also harmful, creates false equivalencies and therefore feeds racial illiteracy. Further, it stops us from tackling structural issues.'

The terms 'racism' and 'prejudice' are not interchangeable, and to remove the element of power from the definition of racism is overly

Why white people can't experience racism

'White people can indeed face stereotypical assumptions based on their skin colour and hence encounter racial prejudice. But this cannot be called racism, because of the inherent systemic imbalance of power between those with lighter skin colour and people of colour.

Racial prejudice can affect people on an individual level, but it would not have the same effect on a larger social and cultural level because it is only when stereotypes are bolstered by power, such as through a eurocentric model of thinking, that it creates systemic and structural racism and oppression that people of colour have encountered throughout history.'

– Dr Pragya Agarwal, author and behavioural scientist

simplistic and ignores the real and damaging impact racism has on the lives of ethnic minorities.

What is 'reverse racism'?

'Reverse racism' is the concept that the dominant racial group in a society – white people – can experience racism at the hands of minority groups.

People of colour can be accused of 'reverse racism' when they carve out safe spaces for themselves. For example, a 'black girls fitness club' might be accused of 'reverse racism' for not including white people in their group.

But most race academics regard 'reverse racism' as a myth. They say it doesn't exist because of the one-way nature of those all-important power structures mentioned above.

The theoretical 'black girls fitness club' is necessary because white people are, by default, welcome in any fitness group,

whereas black women may feel excluded or unwelcome in spaces where they are a minority. That is the difference.

White American activist Tim Wise explains it really succinctly in a 2002 essay: '"n*gger" was and is a term used by whites to dehumanise blacks, to imply their inferiority, to "put them in their place" if you will, the same cannot be said of "honky": after all, you can't put white people in their place when they own the place to begin with.

'Power is like body armour,' Tim continues. 'And while not all white folks have the same degree of power, there is a very real extent to which all of us have more than we need vis-à-vis people of colour: at least when it comes to racial position, privilege and perceptions.'

It isn't hard to understand why some people may argue for the existence of 'reverse racism'. Most white people will face hardships and struggles, and the privileges that come with whiteness aren't in any way a guarantee of an easy life.

So, to some, to say that white people cannot experience racism implies that all white people have an easy life. But that's not what it means at all.

It does not mean that white people don't have struggles, or face prejudice, discrimination or any other kind of hardship. It simply means that when it comes to racism specifically, the structures of society mean white people will always hold more power than people of colour.

9 March 2020

Is antisemitism a form of racism?

Antisemitism means hatred of Jews. The word first appeared in the 19th century, when classification of people into different races was considered normal. Many people in Europe thought the 'white race' was better than other races. But do Jews belong to a separate 'race'? And is antisemitism racism?

Racism is based on the idea that there are different human races: the 'white race', the 'black race', the 'yellow race', and the 'red race'. People of the same race are assumed to share certain characteristics.

Hitler and the National Socialists (Nazis) also believed that people could be divided into races. And they believed that the races were in competition with each other. According to the Nazis, the Jews were a weak, dangerous, and inferior race that did not belong in Germany.

The ideas of Hitler and the Nazis were racist. After the Second World War, science showed that the classification of humanity into different races is wrong. There is only one race: the human race.

Other forms of antisemitism may not be racist, or less so. In the past, hatred against Jews was often fuelled by the Christian churches. Throughout the history of Christian Europe and the Islamic world, there have been times when Jews were persecuted.

People turned against them, not because they belonged to another 'race', but because they did not believe in the right God.

Conclusion: Jews are not a race, and categorising people according to race is wrong and dangerous. Even so, some people still believe in the concept. If it is the basis for their hatred of Jews, it is undoubtedly racist.

6 November 2018

Think racism hasn't affected me? It's there almost every day

From being followed by security guards, to photographers adjusting my skin tone — things have to change.

By Dina Asher-Smith

The past few weeks have been hard for me. In the weeks immediately after George Floyd's murder it was hard. Hard to focus. Hard to sleep. Tiring, exhausting, and emotionally draining. It was heartbreaking.

I've been sad, frustrated, angry. It has been hard to think about it, but also impossible not to. Hard to talk about it but also the only topic that seemed worthy of conversation.

Most of all it was hard to put pen to paper, or fingers to keys, and write something.

I intended for this column to go out weeks ago but I couldn't express myself clearly. I applaud all those who have been able to speak eloquently on a topic so close to our hearts in the midst of emotional turmoil. It has been traumatic.

Sadly, I know that some people will read that and roll their eyes. Or think, "I'm sick of hearing about this", or "here they go again". And yes, whilst some may be sick of hearing about it, black people are sick of having to talk about it, of seeing a brutal murder trend on social media and knowing that it's only trending because someone was able to record it on a smartphone. Black people are sick of being treated differently due to the colour of our skin.

I agreed to be a columnist to take up space. I firmly believe that there are a number of ways to effect change, and one of them is that you have to step outside your own echo chamber and away from people who are naturally inclined to agree with you, and engage those with a different world view.

And whilst many of you will have been profoundly affected by George Floyd, the Black Lives Matter movement and the events of the past few weeks in general I am well aware that some will think, "Dina why were you so upset by this? Why does this warrant space in your sports column? Why are we talking about this in the UK?"

It's because it affects my life too. These few weeks have been so hard for so many people for a number of different reasons. For me, it was because it brought up so many suppressed memories and restated that it doesn't matter what I do or accomplish, how kind or "good" a person I may be, how educated or well-intentioned I am, there are people out there that seek to do me wrong because of the colour of my skin. There are layers and layers of "unconscious" bias at best, and hate at worst, that affect my life on a day-to-day basis.

It's being assumed that I am an employee rather than an attendee at a black-tie event.

It's being assumed that I come from a single-parent household and having consistently to emphasise that yes,

my father is present and does come to my races... yes he's over there... and yes, he is loving and supportive, he has been since the day I was born. It's having to smile through the shocked "Oh" that follows that. It's being followed around not so inconspicuously by security in a store from the moment you step in. It's being assumed you can't afford to buy anything in a nice shop.

It's turning up for a photo shoot and being told your hair was too "Bronx" in cornrows, so it had to be completely restyled. It's having my skin tone lightened in post-production after a shoot had concluded, to such an extent that when I saw the final images I went and looked in the mirror to confirm that I wasn't imagining things.

It's turning up at Stansted airport just a few summers ago, having left your make-up bag at home and not being able to find a single foundation in your shade to replace it – not in duty free, Boots, any store in the entire airport, and having to endure the uncomfortable shuffles of staff moving away as they realise what you're looking for but they know they don't stock anything for you.

It's as a dark-skinned black woman having to undergo the common journey of learning to love your hair the way it grows out of your head and your skin tone in your early twenties as you had grown up with images and the paradigm of beauty as the exact opposite to what you were and messages specifically telling you that in real life exchanges, in music lyrics and from even the dolls you played with at a young age.

In sport it is hearing that a journalist at our World Championships holding camp press day only asked the black male athletes if they had ever been in a gang, had ever seen someone get stabbed and other harmful racial tropes, clearly looking to put the story on to the athlete before the athlete had the chance to show who they were themselves. It's hearing the term "the Africans" used to lazily collectively describe athletes in the distance races – why not use their actual names? – and then seeing debates that the races are hard to follow and not always appealing to a European audience because everyone "looks the same".

It's seeing the black footballers having to endure vile racist chants, Nazi salutes and having banana skins thrown at them, then being criticised for reacting to it and the organisations responsible being given only a minor penalty fine. It's coming on social media and seeing that Ian Wright has yet again opened his Instagram DM's to racial slurs and monkey emojis.

It's thinking about why Serena Williams and Beyoncé almost died in childbirth, that even in the UK black women are five times more likely to die in childbirth than white women. It's why it's not shocking to the BAME community that we are twice as likely to die from coronavirus, because "unconscious" bias, systemic racism and structural inequality express themselves in health crises. It's why the black community isn't shocked that Alexandra Burke was advised to lighten her skin to appeal to the British audience.

And why we were not shocked at the inaction that initially followed George Floyd's murder and the subsequent police brutality we all saw on social media at the protests afterwards. It's why we weren't shocked to see the Buffalo police claim that the 75-year-old man "tripped and fell" despite us all seeing clear as day that he was pushed and left to bleed on the floor. It's not right. It's horrible and wrong, but this is most definitely not new.

I could go on with countless more examples of overt racism and microaggressions, but you know what? It hurts to remember all these things. I am normally a happy, bubbly person, that's the natural disposition of myself and my parents. But sometimes it takes a lot of effort to get there. As my friend Clara Amfo said in her interview with Grazia last week: black joy is a form of resistance – being a joyous black person is radical.

I also don't want to make myself a target. Speaking out is scary. You may get branded as "complaining" and then life gets considerably worse, as experienced by Eniola Aluko who went through so much to fight for justice.

My hope, the same as many who have spoken out recently, is that in writing this column I help to raise awareness and bring about change.

It has been good to see the veil being lifted for many people these last few weeks. It's good that more people feel able to have these conversations and stand up against racism without fear of a backlash or losing their jobs. Let's think about changing the way we talk about people who speak out, let's think about the language we all use in these circumstances. What on earth is an "anti-racist critic"?

We were taught not to use double negatives in primary school, so why is this term being legitimised? Let's say it as it is. I am not thinking of having children any time soon, but when I am ready for that I don't want my son to have to think twice before buying a nice car out of his hard-earned money, as having a nicer car would make him 40 times more likely to be stopped by the police. And I don't want my daughter to have to go through the same "self-love" journey that so many of us are going through right now, or to be branded "aggressive", "scary" or a "diva" for simply expressing her opinion in circumstances she has the right to, like every other human being.

I don't want to have to give my children the same "talk" my parents had to give me at four years old – never let anyone call you certain names, never even look in your bag for a tissue when you are browsing in a store just in case people think you are stealing, and understand you will have to work at least twice as hard, be twice as good, a model of perfection, in order to attain half the recognition, respect and opportunity.

How do we get there? Education is key. We don't learn enough about world history, colonial history and the fact that race is a social construct. We don't teach our children how to be anti-racist at school. I studied history at university because I wanted to understand more about the past, so I had the ability to understand the present and critically think about the future. In that first term of studying my mind was blown. We have to do a better job of accurately educating our children about our history and difficult topics.

We are not equipping our children to understand fully the modern world and the challenges it poses. Whether we like it or not, we are global citizens and that will increase with each generation as the traditional barriers of travel, borders and language are changing. Technology is connecting us like never before, so that you can see a live stream of events in New Zealand or the United States from your phone in Bromley.

Increasingly we communicate through non-verbal means such as hilarious memes and viral dances that emphasise the similarities between us and not the differences.

We are all in a philosophical, reflective mood going through this collective traumatic event of coronavirus. The past few months have been illuminating for so many. It's highlighted how precious and transient life is, exposed shortcomings when it comes to protecting society's most vulnerable and shown us unequal and ineffective systems.

We know how the power of one action, how one person, has the opportunity to change the world. Please stand up and speak out against racism. Be anti-racist. Even if you think that you can't effect change, you can. We all hold influence and whether that's across our dinner tables, in a boardroom or on a platform that millions listen to, it all counts. We all have the power to bring about positive change. Life as we know it has changed so much recently, and many have had to sit back and think about what really matters.

Equality matters. Black Lives Matter.

25 June 2020

Explainer: what is systemic racism and institutional racism?

By Mary Frances O'Dowd

THE CONVERSATION

At the 2020 BAFTA awards, Joaquin Phoenix called out systemic racism in the film industry in his acceptance speech for leading actor.

He said:

I think that we send a very clear message to people of colour that you're not welcome here. I think that's the message that we're sending to people that have contributed so much to our medium and our industry and in ways that we benefit from. [...]

I think it's more than just having sets that are multicultural. We have to do really the hard work to truly understand systemic racism.

"Systemic racism", or "institutional racism", refers to how ideas of white superiority are captured in everyday thinking at a systems level: taking in the big picture of how society operates, rather than looking at one-on-one interactions.

These systems can include laws and regulations, but also unquestioned social systems.

Systemic racism can stem from education, hiring practices or access.

In the case of Phoenix at the BAFTAs, he isn't calling out the racist actions of individuals, but rather the way white is considered the default at every level of the film industry.

Stokely Carmichael and Charles V. Hamilton first wrote about the concept in their 1967 book Black Power: The Politics of Liberation.

They wrote:

When a black family moves into a home in a white neighborhood and is stoned, burned or routed out, they are victims of an overt act of individual racism which most people will condemn. But it is institutional racism that keeps black people locked in dilapidated slum tenements, subject to the daily prey of exploitative slumlords, merchants, loan sharks and discriminatory real estate agents. The society either pretends it does not know of this latter situation, or is in fact incapable of doing anything meaningful about it.

Invisible systems

Systemic racism assumes white superiority individually, ideologically and institutionally. The assumption of superiority can pervade thinking consciously and unconsciously.

One most obvious example is apartheid, but even with anti-discrimination laws, systemic racism continues.

Individuals may not see themselves as racist, but they can still benefit from systems that privilege white faces and voices.

Anti-racism activist Peggy McIntosh popularised the understanding of the systemic nature of racism with her famous "invisible knapsack" quiz looking at white privilege.

The quiz asks you to count how many statements you agree with, for items such as:

♦ I can turn on the television or open to the front page of the paper and see people of my race widely represented

♦ I can be pretty sure of having my voice heard in a group in which I am the only member of my race

♦ I can worry about racism without being seen as self-interested or self-seeking.

The statements highlight taken-for-granted privileges, and enable people to understand how people of colour may experience society differently.

Cultures of discrimination

Under systemic racism, systems of education, government and the media celebrate and reward some cultures over others.

In employment, names can influence employment opportunities. A Harvard study found job candidates were more likely to get an interview when they "whitened" their name.

Only 10% of black candidates got interview offers when their race could be implied by their resume, but 25% got offers when their resumes were whitened. And 21% of Asian candidates got interview offers with whitened resumes, up from 11.5%.

Systemic racism shows itself in who is disproportionately impacted by our justice system. In Australia, Indigenous people make up 2% of the Australian population, but 28% of the adult prison population.

A study into how systemic racism impacts this over-representation in Victoria named factors such as over-policing in Aboriginal communities, the financial hardship of bail, and increased rates of drug and alcohol use.

Australia's literature, theatres and art galleries are all disproportionately white, with less than 10% of artistic directors from culturally diverse backgrounds.

A way forward

Systemic racism damages lives, restricting access and capacity for contribution.

It damages the ethical society we aspire to create.

When white people scoop all the awards, it reinforces a message that other cultures are just not quite good enough.

Public advocacy is critical. Speaking up is essential.

Racism is more than an individual issue. When systemic injustices remain unspoken or accepted, an unethical white privilege is fostered. When individuals and groups point out systemic injustices and inequities, the dominant culture is made accountable.

Find out if your children's school curriculum engages with Indigenous and multicultural perspectives. Question if your university course on Australian literature omits Aboriginal authors. Watch films and read books by artists who don't look like you.

As Phoenix put it in his speech:

I'm part of the problem. […] I think it is the obligation of the people that have created and perpetuate and benefit from a system of oppression to be the ones that dismantle it. That's on us.

Understanding systemic racism is important. To identify these systemic privileges enables us to embrace the point of view of people whose cultures are silenced or minimised.

When we question systemic racism, worth is shared and ideas grow.

5 February 2020

'Institutional racism': 20 years since Stephen Lawrence inquiry

Sir William Macpherson's phrase has fallen out of favour but has Britain really changed?

By Robert Booth, Social affairs correspondent.

Twenty years after Sir William Macpherson was picked to lead the public inquiry into Stephen Lawrence's murder and the allegedly corrupt police investigation that followed, Grenfell Tower went up in flames.

In his final report, published in February 1999, Macpherson would go on to label the police response to the teenager's killing "institutionally racist", a term that captured so well the unwitting prejudice and plain racial stereotyping afflicting parts of British society. The phrase became a lodestar for anti-racism and equality reforms launched in an effort to move the country on from sporadic race riots, racist violence and everyday prejudice of the "no blacks, no dogs, no Irish" variety. There were murmurs Britain was becoming a post-racial society.

Then last September came a discordant clang. A lawyer for some Grenfell families said the public inquiry must ask if the 72 deaths were "a product of institutional racism". At least 34 victims were nationals of African, Middle Eastern or Asian countries. Imran Khan, who represented the Lawrence family to Macpherson, now wanted to know if, 20 years on, unwitting actions had delivered a racist outcome and if institutional racism had affected the way firefighters behaved.

The phrase, once described as "incendiary" by Trevor Philips, the former chair of the Equality and Human Rights Commission (EHRC), was back. It was an offensive slur, said firefighters, who had shown bravery, saved lives and witnessed horrors. But it had to be asked because the demise

of institutional racism cannot be assumed even though it has fallen out of favour in preference to the softer language of "unconscious bias". It was clear when the former Labour MP, Angela Smith, this week described ethnicity as "a funny tinge", even people you would expect to show confidence on the matter still struggle to talk about race.

Macpherson defined institutional racism as "the collective failure of an organisation to provide an appropriate and professional service to people because of their colour, culture or ethnic origin". It is seen in "processes, attitudes and behaviour which amount to discrimination through unwitting prejudice, ignorance, thoughtlessness and racist stereotyping which disadvantages minority ethnic people".

Two decades on, statistics collated in the government's race disparity audit – one sign of progress itself perhaps – tell part of the story.

The number of black and Caribbean pupils achieving 5 A*-C GCSE grades including maths and English increased from 34% in 2006 to nearly 49% in 2012, a larger rise than for white British pupils. The number of minority ethnic students at top universities rose from 9% in 1995 to 18% in 2017. But gulfs remain. In 2016-17, 3.6% of black Caribbean A-level students got three top grades or better compared with 11.2% of whites. Only one black British student was admitted to Corpus Christi College, Oxford in 2015, 2016 and 2017 collectively.

More mixed race people than white people were victims of crime last year; white offenders were given the shortest custodial sentences from 2009 to 2017 and black people are detained under the Mental Health Act four times more often than white people.

All ethnic groups have a higher proportion of people living in overcrowded homes than white British people (2%), with the most overcrowded being among Bangladeshis (30%). Home ownership remains far higher for whites than ethnic minorities, who are also twice as likely to be unemployed.

There are some upsides. Black people are more likely to have cancer diagnosed earlier, are more likely to be involved in local decision-making and ethnic minorities are more likely to use the internet. The first minority ethnic mayors have been elected in London and Bristol and Sajid Javid has become the first minority ethnic home secretary.

Nevertheless, Stephen Lawrence's mother, Doreen, said this month progress reforming institutions was "stagnant".

"As time moved on, it's as though they changed the word from 'racism' to diversity, and then 'diversity doesn't exist any more'," Lady Lawrence told MPs. On the 10th anniversary of the Macpherson report, Philips had said it was no longer true to describe the police as institutionally racist – citing Merseyside police's handling of the investigation into the racist murder of another black teenager Anthony Walker in 2005. But last month, Lawrence said some police officers still were.

What is certainly true is that none of the forces operating in England and Wales reflect the population they serve. Fourteen percent of the population is non-white, compared with 6.6% of the police forces. In London, where the minority population is 40%, only 14% of officers are from that group.

Dr Pete Jones, a psychologist who has run more than 2,000 implicit bias tests for police forces, found almost a fifth of officers and police staff tested since 2009 have an ethnicity bias strong enough to impact their behaviour.

So perhaps it is no surprise that last week the EHRC warned of "persistent racial inequalities" in stop and search, traffic stops, use of force and deaths during and after police contact.

Twelve percent of incidents when police use force against people involve black people, despite them only making up 3.3% of the population and race hate crimes were up 14% in the year to 2017/18 (though police reporting improvements are likely to be a factor).

Omar Khan, the director of the Runnymede Trust, a race equality thinktank, also highlights the recently emboldened far right, Labour's response to antisemitism in the party and the disproportionate effect of welfare cuts on minorities as evidence of continued problems.

"There has been a lack of recognition over the last 20 years about how far behind we have been," he said. "We still tiptoe around racism. It makes most people uncomfortable talking about it today."

Nevertheless, Matthew Ryder QC, until recently London's deputy mayor for integration, believes the change Macpherson has wrought on society is "so significant we have almost forgotten what it was like before".

"The notion that there was a structural component to racism that is more impactful than personal animus or hostility is now well established," he said. "That was almost a completely alien concept before the Stephen Lawrence inquiry happened.

"The current settlement between ethnic minorities and society as a whole in modern Britain, and the way we articulate and understand the nature of racism, has been largely set by the Stephen Lawrence inquiry."

He said it empowered black people to hold institutions to account for racism but said there were signs of backsliding in some "stubborn" areas, for example in the calls for more stop and search to tackle knife crime. Some black youth do believe it is a suitable deterrent, it happens less frequently

than at any time since the turn of the millennium and is more likely to result in arrest. But black people are more than eight times more likely to be stopped than whites, and the disparity is rising, increasing criticism that it is a tool of racial discrimination and may even be counter-productive.

Kalwant Bhopal, a Birmingham University professor of education and social justice and author of White privilege: the myth of a post-racial society, said that since Macpherson the race equality agenda has been "pushed into insignificance".

"If the Race Relations Amendment Act (2000) and Macpherson were effective why is it that if you are a black student you are less likely to leave university with a 2:1 or a first, less likely to attend an elite university and are more likely to be unemployed six months after graduation?" she said.

In 2019, Bhopal believes "white privilege" still dominates society with policy makers, employers and others in power only advancing racial justice if it supports their own interests. They create "a smokescreen of conformity" with race equality agendas, she said, concluding: "We seem to be going round in circles".

22 February 2019

Home Office showed 'institutional ignorance and thoughtlessness' towards race, Windrush report finds

Department's attitude towards race issues and history of Windrush generation 'consistent with some elements of the definition of institutional racism', says inspector of constabulary Wendy Williams in long-awaited report.

By May Bulman, Social affairs corresponden.t

The Home Office has demonstrated "institutional ignorance and thoughtlessness" towards the issue of race, an independent report into the Windrush scandal has revealed.

The review, commissioned after people with a right to live in the UK were wrongfully detained or deported to the Caribbean, finds that those affected were let down by "systemic operational failings".

Its publication has prompted calls for an independent review specifically into the extent of institutional racism in the Home Office and whether its immigration policies are in line with equality law.

In a damning indictment of the Home Office, inspector of constabulary Wendy Williams, the report's author, stated

that the fiasco, which saw people with a right to live in the UK wrongfully detained or deported to the Caribbean, was "foreseeable and avoidable".

She said: "Warning signs from inside and outside the Home Office were simply not heeded by officials and ministers. Even when stories of members of the Windrush generation being affected by the immigration control started to emerge in the media from 2017 onwards, the department was slow to react."

Ms Williams accused successive governments of trying to demonstrate they were being tough on immigration by tightening immigration control and passing laws creating and then expanding the "hostile environment", with a "complete disregard" for the Windrush generation.

The report identifies organisational factors in the Home Office which created the operating environment in which the mistakes could be made, including a "culture of disbelief and carelessness" when dealing with immigration applications.

It concludes that the Windrush scandal showed "institutional ignorance and thoughtlessness" on race issues which is "consistent with some elements of the definition of institutional racism".

Speaking in the House of Commons yesterday, home secretary Priti Patel accepted that there were "structural and cultural" issues in the Home Office, and gave an official apology.

"There is nothing I can say today that will undo the suffering ... On behalf of this and successive governments I am truly sorry," she told MPs.

Labour MP David Lammy said the review was a "brutal indictment" of the Home Office which showed it was "wholly unfit" for the society it is supposed to serve.

"The review shows the Windrush scandal was not an innocent mistake, but a systemic pattern of appalling behaviour rooted in a toxic internal culture and a failure of the department to understand Britain's colonial history," he said.

"When the problem is institutional, the only solution is to tear out the ruined foundations and rebuild the institution brick by brick. This is what the Home Office needs."

Mr Lammy called on the Home Office to end the hostile environment immediately, create a new purpose and culture at the department based on the rule of law, openness and diversity, and fundamentally rebuild the Home Office.

He added that it was unfortunate that the report had been published in the midst of the coronavius emergency, saying it was "hard to imagine a worse time" for it to be published.

"For the sake of all those black British citizens who were deported, detained, made homeless, jobless, denied healthcare housing and welfare by their own government, we cannot allow this news to be buried."

Ms Williams said both ministers and officials in the Home Office must learn lessons from the scandal, saying ministers set the policy and the direction of travel and did not sufficiently question unintended consequences, while officials could and should have done more to examine, consider and explain the impacts of decisions.

Outlining specific changes and improvements, she said the department must acknowledge the wrong which has been done, open itself up to greater external scrutiny; and it must change its culture to recognise that migration and wider Home Office policy is about people and, whatever its objective, should be rooted in humanity.

The inspector of constabulary also called for a full review and evaluation of the hostile environment policy and the creation of a "migrants commissioner responsible for speaking up for migrants and those affected by the system".

In response to the review's findings, a group of race equality and migrant rights organisations have called for an independent review into the extent of institutional racism in the Home Office and whether its immigration policies are in line with equality law around racial discrimination.

Dr Zubaida Haque, deputy director of the Runnymede Trust, said it was now "incumbent" on this government to understand "how and why Home Office culture, attitudes, immigration and citizenship policies have repeatedly discriminated against black and ethnic minority British citizens".

"Unless the issues around institutional racism are meaningfully addressed, we risk the same mistakes and injustices being repeated," she said. Ms Patel said she would bring forward a detailed formal response in the next six months, as Wendy Williams has recommended, representing a "new chapter" for the Home Office.

"Let me assure this house that everyone at the Home Office will be asking the difficult questions needed to ensure that these circumstances can never arise again," she added. Since the scandal emerged in 2018, more than 8,000 have been given "some form of documentation" and the immigration status has been confirmed for almost 2,500, according to the most recent figures from the Home Office.

The department identified 164 people who had been deported or put in detention since 2002 amid the Windrush scandal, records said.

A compensation scheme with an estimated budget of at least £200m has been set up, but campaigners have hit out at the "paltry" number of people who have so far received payments, describing the process as "slow and onerous".

19 March 2020

Microaggressions are not a 'harmless' form of racism – they have a huge impact

Racism comes in many forms, but there are two key categories – overt and covert.

By Natalie Morris

Overt racism is the obvious, undeniable stuff. The 'n-word', the 'p-word', the aggressive, openly hostile stuff.

Covert is sneakier, harder to pinpoint, harder to call out. This is the category microaggressions fall in to, and many people of colour in this country experience them on a daily basis.

On their own, microaggressions may not seem like much, and they can be easy to brush off in isolation – but the accumulative effect of brushing off multiple microaggressions, every day, can be draining, demoralising and utterly disheartening.

What is a microaggression?

A microaggression is an instance of subtle, indirect discrimination against a marginalised group. It doesn't always have to be about race – they can be based on gender, sexuality and physical ability too – but they are commonly experienced by racial minorities.

The dictionary says that microaggressions can be 'unintentional' – but the intention doesn't change the effects that these actions and statements have on people of colour.

Examples of microaggressions

Leah, 24

'I was called the wrong name by the receptionist in my office every day for sixth months. She just wouldn't learn my name. This didn't happen with any of my white colleagues.

'The first few times I told her what my name was, but after about a month I just had to stop trying because it was too awkward.'

James, 33

'I was at a Christmas party and one of my colleagues (drunkenly) came over to me and just put their hands in my hair. I have short Afro hair, and this person rubbed my head and said I felt like a sheep.

'I jerked my head away, but just kind of smiled awkwardly and snuck off to the bar. I didn't fancy making a scene because I didn't think anyone would back me up.'

Iqra, 26

'This was at a work event – I was giving a talk and afterwards, one of the people who had been in the crowd came up to me. He was an older white man.

'He said to me; "you were so eloquent and well-spoken. Is English your first language?"

'I just stared at him. What a question to ask! I wanted to ask if he had ever assumed that of his white colleagues. But I didn't, of course.'

Jeanette, 32

'I'm mixed-race and I am constantly asked – "no, where are you really from?" It may seem innocuous,

or like it's not a big deal, but being asked that all the time makes it feel like you don't belong anywhere.

'You wouldn't ask a white person that. What you're really asking me is – "why do you look different?"'

The tricky thing about microaggressions is that individually, they are perceived as small.

They are daily, commonplace interactions that can't always be readily identified as racism by people who have little experience of it.

This puts minorities who experience microaggressions in a tough position, as to speak out about a seemingly 'small' incident can be viewed as disproportionate. Many people worry about being perceived as aggressive, angry or as 'playing the race card'.

The impact of these microaggressions is that the people who experience them are often left feeling powerless and afraid to speak out – particularly in the workplace, or out of fear of making friendships or professional relationships awkward.

It's actually not a new term. It was coined by Harvard University professor Chester M. Pierce in the 1970s.

'These assaults to black dignity and black hope are incessant and cumulative,' he wrote.

'Any single one may be gross. In fact, the major vehicle for racism in this country is offences done to blacks by whites in this sort of gratuitous neverending way. These offences are microaggressions.'

He added that almost all racial interactions between black people and white people are characterised by these automatic and unconscious put-downs from white people.

'These mini disasters accumulate,' he says. 'It is the sum total of multiple microaggressions by whites to blacks that has pervasive effect to the stability and peace of this world.'

What are the effects of microaggressions?

Research has consistently shown just how damaging microaggressions can be for people who experience them regularly.

A 2018 study in the Journal of Multicultural Counseling and Development found that of counsellors who had clients reporting race-based trauma, 89% identified 'covert acts of racism' as a contributing factor.

The commonplace, subtle nature of microaggressions can also have a significant detrimental impact on the health of people of colour who experience them.

Research has provided strong evidence that microaggressions lead to higher levels of depression and trauma. In one US study of 405 students at an undergraduate university, depressive symptoms were the link in the relationship between racial microaggressions and thoughts of suicide.

In another recent study of Native Americans with diabetes, a correlation was found between microaggressions and self-reported histories of heart attack, depressive symptoms, and prior-year hospitalisation.

Despite the name, these instances of racism are not small enough to be harmless. The impact and accumulative trauma is real and can be anything but 'micro'.

It's easy to dismiss microaggressions as less damaging than more overt forms of racism, but the regularity that minorities are confronted with these subtle forms of prejudice means the impact can be worse than more obvious, but less frequent, forms of racial hostility.

Everyone needs to do better in identifying and calling out microaggressions wherever they see them. And support minorities when they report this kind of racism because it's isolating to have to fight these tiny battles, alone, every single day.

13 March 2020

The leaked Labour report reveals a shocking level of racism and sexism towards its black MPs

The messages about Dawn Butler and Diane Abbott are a visceral reminder of the discrimination black women face in the workplace.

By Yomi Adegoke

Many black British women feel a particular, protective kind of kinship toward black female MPs, grateful for their representation both figuratively and literally in the face of media attacks.

So the leak of an internal report from Labour HQ, which alleges senior staff exhibiting the very prejudice they claim to fight against, has been especially hard to digest.

The 860-page document has unearthed a plethora of party horrors: allegations of misuse of funds, the continued undermining of the 2017 electoral campaign and the then-leader Jeremy Corbyn's attempts to investigate anti-Semitism in the party, as well as vicious criticism of leading Labour figures by staff members in private messages.

The entire dossier is hard to swallow, but the messages regarding Dawn Butler and Diane Abbott left a singularly bitter aftertaste.

One staff member "engaged in a classic racist trope" by referring to the Hackney North MP as an "angry woman", while another called her "repulsive."

When Ms Abbott was found crying in the toilets in the wake of abuse in 2017, a female staff member suggested telling a Channel 4 journalist of her whereabouts. Another replied that he already had, followed by a wink emoji.

One can only fathom the level of dehumanisation that has taken place, for peers to gleefully relish in bullying that has brought a colleague to the brink and then contribute to it.

Society still fails to fully acknowledge the scourges of sexism and racism, but we are miles from reckoning with misogynoir – a combination of both that doubly penalises black women in distinct ways.

It is why Ms Butler was once mistaken for a cleaner by another MP.

It is why, while female MPs received disproportionate abuse in the six weeks before the last general election, Diane Abbott alone received almost half of all the abusive tweets sent.

The report is just a visible and visceral reminder about what black women often have to face within the workplace – or in this case, politics. Attacks that hinge on your identity are not just likely from the expected groups – opposing parties, the press – but must be anticipated from your own colleagues.

Even if on you're on the same political side, many also ally with white supremacy and sexism.

Several black women can relate to instances outlined in the documents from breakdowns in the loos to facing contempt for speaking out against discrimination.

The report showed two female staff members deriding Ms Butler's anti-racism in a mocking set of messages. "Did she not accuse the LP and it's staff of being racist this week? Nice," read one.

If Labour members are scoffing at the issues Ms Butler raises regarding racism, then who do we turn to to fight inequality?

Those who privately pour scorn on our concerns or those who do so publicly, such as Boris Johnson, who once casually referred to black people as "piccaninnies" in a newspaper column?

In response to this report, we need a stronger sign of solidarity from the party which has let down black female MPs so terribly.

13 July 2020

Gypsy, Roma and Traveller communities endure worsening racism and inequality: this must be a turning point

An article from The Conversation.

By Philip Brown, University of Salford

THE CONVERSATION

Gypsy, Roma and Traveller communities continue to experience open discrimination and prejudice, both in the UK and Europe. Just in the past few weeks Roma people have been attacked in France as a result of fake news spread about the community. Meanwhile in the UK, the Equality and Human Rights Commission intervened in a holiday park which held a "no Travellers" rule, and a caravan site allocated for use for Travellers was subject to an arson attack.

April 8, 2019 marks International Roma Day – a day created to celebrate Romani culture and raise awareness of the issues facing Roma people. The day was established in 1990, but since this time the challenges Roma face have remained and even increased, driven by the rise of the Far Right and austerity.

The reality of their situation has been driven home by a new report from the House of Commons Women and Equalities Committee, which provides a damning critique of the progress made on addressing the inequalities faced by Gypsy, Roma and Traveller communities. It also challenges the government to do more to improve communities' outcomes in education and health care, [and] tackle discrimination and hate crime, as well as violence against women and girls.

The committee report demands that the government develop a clear and effective plan to support Gypsy, Roma and Traveller communities, in line with the inequalities they face. The report also suggests a key role can be played by the Race Disparity Unit, which gathers information on the experiences of minority groups in the UK, by demanding that government departments must "explain or change" any disparities between Gypsy, Roma and Traveller communities and the general population.

A history of neglect

The fact is, the discrimination and adverse life chances faced by Gypsy, Roma and Traveller populations in the UK and Europe have been a problem for decades. Reports from the Commission for Racial Equality (in 2006), the Equality and Human Rights Commission (in 2010) and the European Commission (in 2018) have rigorously documented the inequalities and discrimination faced by these communities.

Indeed, the most recent of these confirmed that countries with larger Roma populations experienced an increase in anti-Roma hate speech, segregated and poor accommodation, even as hundreds of thousands of Roma endured a lack of access to basic services including clean water and sanitation. With the steady arrival of Roma from central and eastern Europe to the UK, there's a real risk of replicating the hostile anti-Roma environment seen in much of central and eastern Europe, which forces such communities to flee and polarises neighbourhoods.

The UK government's record on Roma issues has been one of inaction and neglect. Plans such as the coalition's 2012 strategy to tackle inequalities have been widely derided for having limited scope, little ambition and weak recommendations. The most recent inquiry failed to consider the shortage of pitches and site accommodation across the UK, which many groups representing Roma, Gypsy and Traveller communities would consider to be one of the most pressing concerns.

Yet the report represents a significant intervention against government inaction and hostile policy making. Few politicians – with notable exceptions such as Kate Green and Baroness Whitaker – speak out against the inequalities faced by Gypsy, Roma and Traveller communities. Indeed, during the inquiry, Conservative MP Jackie Doyle-Price said: "Let's be honest: we are all Members of Parliament and we all know there are no votes in championing this group of people".

As with all reports prepared by parliamentary committees, the government has 40 days to respond. With the current atmosphere of anti-migrant sentiment in the UK, coupled with the continuing hostility to Gypsies and Travellers, it is difficult to predict the sort of response the report will receive. But maintaining the status quo cannot be an option.

Turning point

Gypsy, Roma and Traveller communities, on average, continue to die far younger than members of other communities and have poorer health than members of other communities. They also experience the death of a child far more frequently than other communities. The needs and position of Gypsy, Roma and Traveller communities are so stark that considered steps must be taken.

So this should be an opportunity for the government and other public bodies to take more forceful and co-ordinated action. One way forward is for the government to use the Race Disparity Audit to address inequalities. Vocal leadership is also required from within government at all levels. For too long, Gypsy, Roma and Traveller communities have been used as a political football, with few people in positions of power speaking up for their needs.

Successive governments have tried doing nothing, pilot projects have been attempted and mainstreaming the needs of Gypsy, Roma and Traveller communities has been the recent approach. But all have failed over the long term or led to very little improvement. Government needs to lead and to foster leadership in others – there needs to be coordinated plans and actions. As in most areas, resources will also be an issue, but a desire and an ability to effect change is critical. In doing so, the UK will address some of the longstanding issues for Gypsy, Roma and Traveller people and make communities more equal and less hostile places.

5 April 2019

University racism inquiry criticised for including anti-white abuse

'Institutions are living in the past and have failed to learn from history,' watchdog warns.

Eleanor Busby, Education correspondent

The equality watchdog has come under fire for including anti-white abuse in its inquiry into racial harassment across UK universities.

Academics and student leaders have criticised the Equality and Human Rights Commission (EHRC) for featuring examples of harassment against white students and staff in their report on racism.

The inquiry found that nearly a quarter (24 per cent) of ethnic minority students experienced racial harassment at a UK university since starting their course, compared to 9 per cent of white students.

The report – which criticised universities for being "oblivious" to the racial harassment occurring at an "alarmingly high rate" on their campuses – also highlighted examples of anti-English sentiment.

White English students and staff in Scottish and Welsh universities had experienced abuse, the inquiry found. One white English member of staff said Welsh colleagues had called him a negative slur for English people.

"I've never come across so much racism as when I moved to Wales," he said.

Fope Olaleye, the black students' officer at the National Union of Students (NUS), claimed that the EHRC had ignored pleas for anti-white harassment to be excluded from their report.

They tweeted: "I remember sitting at one of the round tables and a bunch of students and myself had to explain in excruciating detail that 'anti-white prejudice' should have no place in a report on racial harassment but I see we were not listened to."

Speaking to The Independent, they said: "By conflating xenophobia, Anti-English sentiment and prejudice alongside the racism faced by students of colour in the EHRC report, it has done a disservice to the work currently being done on race equity in the UK."

Priyamvada Gopal, a reader in the faculty of English at Cambridge University, accused the EHRC of placing anti-

English sentiment on par with black students' experiences in white-majority institutions, adding that the report was "dangerous".

Helen Carr, head of equality at the University and College Union, said: "It's unfortunate that the report's inclusion of harassment against white people risks distracting attention from the high levels of racism experienced by BME staff and students.

"To ensure we can tackle these issues effectively, it's important that harassment linked to nationality or immigration status as opposed to ethnicity is explicitly recognised as such."

The inquiry, based on a survey of 1,000 students and interviews with staff, comes after a series of high-profile racist incidents have taken place on UK campuses in recent years.

Black students' experiences have been in the spotlight – with racist chants in student halls and a banana being thrown at a black graduate hitting the headlines.

An investigation by The Independent revealed that the number of racist incidents in universities across the UK surged by more than 60 per cent between 2015 and 2017.

In recent weeks, a University of Leicester student was reported to be pictured wearing a white T-shirt with the hand-written slogan "Hitler wanted my kind alive" during a social event.

Students at the University of Southampton were also filmed chanting racist songs on a bus during a football social, according to student news reports.

The report from the EHRC suggests up to two-thirds of students did not report racist harassment to their university as some had no confidence the incident would be addressed.

Some universities are reluctant to admit the prevalence of racial harassment on campus for fear of reputational damage or putting off potential students, it adds.

Rebecca Hilsenrath, chief executive of EHRC, said: "It is considerably disappointing to discover that, instead of being progressive and forward-thinking, [universities] are living in the past and have failed to learn from history. No one should ever be subjected to racial harassment in any setting.

"Our report reveals that not only are universities out of touch with the extent that this is occurring on their campuses, some are also completely oblivious to the issue. This isn't good enough."

The watchdog is calling on the universities to ensure that students and staff are able to report harassment and that their complaints procedures are fit for purpose.

Earlier this month, a report from Universities UK (UUK) said institutions have been prioritising sexual harassment and gender-based violence but less status has been given to race-based incidents.

At the time, Professor Julia Buckingham, president of UUK, called on university leaders to take "urgent action" over the issues and make it a "top priority".

She said: "There is no place for racial harassment on a university campus, or anywhere else – and I find it sad and shocking how many people are still subject to it. Universities must be places where all students and staff are able to flourish and we must intensify our work to ensure this happens."

On the criticism of the inclusion of anti-white abuse, a spokesperson from the EHRC said: "We have used the definition of race under the Equality Act which includes race, ethnicity and nationality. Our report is very clear that racial harassment predominantly impacts Black and Asian students.

"We received a small number of examples of anti-English sentiment at Scottish and Welsh universities, offensive comments about Gypsy and Irish Traveller students and examples of antisemitic slurs for both staff and students. To ignore these issues raised with us would have been wrong.

"While this is not a form of harassment widely reported to us during the inquiry, there is no place for racial harassment anywhere in society and universities must have systems in place to ensure that everyone can reach their full potential through education. Our recommendations are designed to ensure that universities can appropriately address and tackle racial harassment in all of its forms."

11 November 2019

Time to speak up: some necessary words about racism

By Tracie Jolliff

In September 2016 nine people from Black Lives Matter UK chained themselves together on the runway at London City airport to protest against racial injustice. Seven of them were arrested after passengers complained about inconvenience, and the nation failed to see what the fuss was all about. It's hard to believe that just four years later the world appears to have made an about turn. Today there's not a corner of our globe that has not heard of the Black Lives Matter (BLM) movement. Statues that symbolised the permanence of systems in which racial injustice was the necessary fuel for their operation (slavery, apartheid, colonialism) have been toppled; and personal/collective pledges to be part of this movement for change have been made by people of every hue and in every tongue.

In the wake of this seismic global shift, those who have committed their lives to bringing about social justice are asking, is this the moment that will herald transformation? And as eloquently stated by Martin Luther King Jr, is this the moment when the 'arc of the universe bends toward justice'?

The impact of racism on those from the African and Asian diaspora

The horrific murder of George Floyd still haunts me. I have not watched the videos, I cannot. It was more than enough to see a news bulletin containing a still image of a white police officer, with his hand casually in his pocket, nonchalantly committing murder in front of the cameras, despite pleas from the crowd to stop. He did not care that he was causing harm and appeared to be assured of his right to oppress another in such a cruel and barbaric fashion. This story, however chilling, is not new.

It was my partner's work colleague, a kind and thoughtful white woman who said to him when discussing the lived experiences of racism, as told by people from the African and Asian diaspora in the UK, 'But I don't want to believe that these things are true, and that we live in a world that treats people in such inhumane ways.'

'Conversations [are taking place across the system] about the different perceptions about race and racism, and how racism manifests itself. These conversations in parallel lines are, more often than not, colour coded along the lines of race.'

This statement captures the essence of something significant, a difference that shows up in many conversations that are taking place across the system right now, often in unwavering parallel lines. Conversations about the different perceptions about race and racism, and how racism manifests itself. These conversations in parallel lines are, more often than not, colour coded along the lines of race.

Having raised one's awareness and understanding about race, one cannot fail to have noticed both the consistent pattern of discrimination revealed year on year by the Workforce Race Equality Standard (WRES) scores and the disproportionate impact of Covid-19 on staff from ethnic minorities, with many trusts failing to undertake risk assessments with the urgency required to save lives.

The BLM movement is again starkly underlining what it really means to be a person from the African and Asian diaspora within the NHS. The discomforting feelings this statement may evoke cannot simply be pushed to one side. If Black lives really do matter, we – all of us who work in or with the NHS – need to bravely go where the NHS has not been before, taking a long look into the racialised mirror that begins with the statement, 'We are not all equal'.

The contours of inequity

I am not inclined to sanitise the word racism at this juncture with inclusion. Racism is as harsh as the word suggests, and being on the receiving end of it is alarming, devastating and brutal. Like other forms of injustice it's an act of cruelty, it dehumanises and demeans and suggests the following truth.

Some racial groups thrive because others do not.

'If Black lives really do matter, we – all of us who work in or with the NHS – need to bravely go where the NHS has not been before, taking a long look into the racialised mirror that begins with the statement, 'We are not all equal'.'

This is a difficult correlation to come to terms with. But it is precisely how racism was designed to work, and continues to work very effectively, reproducing unethical power relationships across racial differences.

Racism is enacted daily in a number of ways, and in order to eliminate racism we must first of all see race. In its most subtle forms, race does not even need to be evoked for the behaviours that marginalise to hit their ethnic minority targets. I have observed racism conveyed by:

♦ evoking lazy negative racial stereotypes to label people from ethnic minorities, knowing that these familiar tags are likely to stick

- targeting those who speak out about racism and consistently refusing to support their work; then claiming that the person from an ethnic minority has failed to deliver

- expecting impossible standards of perfection from leaders from ethnic minorities while white leaders who exhibit moral inconsistencies and poor behaviours are not held to similar exacting standards

- isolating leaders from ethnic minorities by not including them in social gatherings

- continually asking leaders from ethnic minorities to prove themselves and to justify their actions

- singling out leaders from ethnic minorities for targeted and sustained criticism

- not recognising the innovation, contributions and talents of leaders from ethnic minorities, at times attributing their hard work to others who happen to be white

- generally treating leaders from ethnic minorities less favourably than their white counterparts

- not calling out colleagues when they denigrate leaders from ethnic minorities in the ways described above.

The viral video of Amy Cooper calling the police on a Black man, who was committing no crime, with the added effects of her contrived trembling voice, spoke about the fact that beneath the politeness and adherence to social taboos, we all know how racism works and which racialised weapons are able to inflict maximum damage. We need to talk more about how racism works, so that good people can see more clearly the contours of the processes that exclude. Choices can then be made not to support these reprehensible processes.

We can be better but we can only move forward if we work together

I say all of this because I believe the NHS – and wider society – can all be much better, if we embrace the truths that we must now grapple with, and we work together to progress racial justice. We are truly on the precipice of moving forward, progressing racial justice and learning what it is to make decisions that decisively reject racism and its operations, in order to embrace antiracist practice and justice.

'We need to talk more about how racism works, so that good people can see more clearly the contours of the processes that exclude. Choices can then be made not to support these reprehensible processes.'

The above is an invitation for us all to take a closer look at what is happening around us. I have watched as the NHS Chief People Officer – a woman of Asian descent – has been subjected to the above behaviours on multiple occasions. This is unacceptable, but I'm also noticing an absence of voices that are speaking out about this.

In a system that claims to recognise that racial disparities, and therefore structural racial discrimination, are embedded into cultures, policies and practices – and has the WRES evidence to prove this – there is a perceptible disconnect between this professed recognition and the system's willingness to call out the very racism it says that it seeks to root out.

I have enjoyed and welcomed the hope-filled conversations of past weeks, but we need to do more. We need to stop tolerating the intolerable, speak truth and call out racism where we see it. In systems where structural racism is the bedrock, leaders from ethnic minorities will be subjected to the kinds of treatment described above. And yes, I'm calling this out.

No human beings are infallible and our leaders from ethnic minorities are as human as the next person, they will fail at things. In those instances, if we embrace justice and offer the gift of honest and thoughtful feedback, we can help these leaders to succeed. On the contrary, if we believe that we can support the BLM movement, racial justice and embrace antiracist practice, without fully supporting the very people that we claim we are seeking to positively impact, we are simply deluding ourselves. Can we really practise a version of racial justice that does not deliver on racial justice? This concept is simply absurd.

> *'...there is a perceptible disconnect between this professed recognition [of recognising racial disparities]... and the system's willingness to call out the very racism it says that it seeks to root out.'*

Our antiracist practice should be positively felt by people from ethnic minorities, and if one is determined not to support the work of leaders from ethnic minorities, this is a stance that requires deeper examination as we should no longer accept the naivety of claims not to see colour. There is no racially neutral fence to sit on, the existence of such a fence is a myth.

Antiracism is our urgent call to action.

Stand against all forms of oppression

Many white leaders have asked me over the past few weeks what they can do to support this global demand for racial justice. This is not a new demand, as those who have been colonised and enslaved, denied freedom, education, jobs, progression and opportunity have been calling out for racial justice for generations before our births. In many ways, the fact that this demand is not new shines a light on some of the much needed actions.

1. The first step is to decide that you are going to support leaders from ethnic minorities. Get behind them, racism is real and we need our colleagues from ethnic minorities, white, LGBT+, those with disabilities and those without, old, young and from all backgrounds to step in with their support. There is also a reciprocity here, we must stand against all forms of oppression, racism is no exception to this.

2. Grow your awareness, educate yourselves, read, scour the internet and learn about the histories that have created our present realities. I am so encouraged by the honesty and integrity of some white colleagues. When you support this agenda I have personally felt your support. Keep going.

3. Notice the racialised macro- and micro-aggressions. Decide not to collude and instead invite your colleagues to examine their behaviours more deeply.

4. Let's adopt the practice of critical self-reflection, asking ourselves continually, to what extent our behaviours are aligning with our values. Advancing racial justice depends on us all making moment-by-moment decisions that support progress. Each time we support progress we create the conditions in which others find it easier to do the same.

Let's speak up and challenge the individuals and cultures in which people feel that they have the right to racially oppress others.

9 July 2020

Joliffe T (2020). 'Time to speak up: some necessary words about racism'. Blog. The King's Fund website.
Available at: www.kingsfund.org.uk/blog/2020/07/necessary-words-racism.

www.kingsfund.org.uk

27,000 fans around the world show attitudes towards race inclusion in football.

In the largest recorded study of its kind, Kick It Out (www.kickitout.org), football's equality and inclusion organisation, and live-score app, Forza Football (www.forzafootball.com), have released a report documenting global attitudes towards issues of racism in football.

With close to 27,000 respondents from 38 different countries, the data report reveals international attitudes towards some of the most significant issues of racial equality within the sport.

Key findings

Globally, over half of football fans (54%) have witnessed racist abuse while watching a football game. Only 28% would know how to appropriately report such racist incidents.

In the UK, more than half of fans have witnessed racist abuse (50%), but less than half would know how to report it (40%). In the US, these figures are 51% and 28% respectively.

61% of fans internationally would support points deductions for national or club teams whose fans are found guilty of racist abuse (for example, Chelsea having points deducted following their game in Paris in 2015).

Globally, 74% of fans want FIFA to consider previous racist abuse when awarding countries international tournaments. The hosts of the 2026 World Cup are in agreement, with 77% of Americans wanting this, 76% of Mexicans, and 77% of Canadians.

In Middle Eastern countries, 80% of fans support this view too. However, problematically ahead of the Qatar World Cup 2022, only 13% of fans from Arabic countries would know how to report incidents of racist abuse.

On average, 84% of fans would feel comfortable with a player of a different ethnic/racial background than them representing their nation or club team.

Fans in Norway (95%), Sweden (94%), and Brazil (93%) feel most comfortable with a player of different ethnic / racial background representing their national or club team. Fans in Saudi Arabia (11%), Lebanon (15%), and the UAE (19%) feel least comfortable.

When it comes to the countries housing the 'Top 5' European leagues, 93% of French people, 92% of Brits, 77% of Germans and Spaniards, and 71% of Italians feel comfortable with a player of different ethnic / racial background representing their national or club team. This figure for the US is 91%.

Lord Ousley, Chair of Kick It Out, comments:

"The research is a timely reminder of both the progress that has been made in tackling racism in football, and the challenges that remain. There is clear global trend towards an acceptance of the BAME community's central role in football, but further progress is unlikely to be made until governing bodies are bolder in their efforts to eradicate racism from every level.

The governing bodies, including The FA, UEFA and FIFA, must do more to promote methods of reporting racism and they must listen to supporters' demands – clubs or countries whose supporters are racially abusive should face harsher sanctions, including points deductions."

Patrik Arnesson, Founder and CEO of Forza Football, comments:

"One mission of our app is to give fans a powerful collective voice, when otherwise they might be ignored. This report shows a real appetite for meaningful change in footballing policy. Organisations such as FIFA need to take note of the number

of fans advocating points deductions for incidents of racism, for example. Our data shows that the footballing world is modernising in relation to certain issues, but that there is also a long way to go."

Christopher Dawes and Daniel Rubenson, Associate Professors in the Politics departments at New York and Ryerson University respectively, who provided methodological advice on the study, comment:

"This is a very impressive data collection effort and an important source of information on racial attitudes among football supporters. The scale of the survey, certainly one of the biggest of its kind, makes it particularly useful for comparing these attitudes across countries and regions."

Extended findings

♦ A higher proportion of fans in Peru (77%), Costa Rica (77%), and Colombia (71%) have witnessed what they would classify as racist abuse while watching football matches, than in anywhere else in the world.

♦ Countries with the smallest proportion of fans having witnessed what they would classify as racist abuse while watching football matches are the Netherlands (38%), Russia (41%), and Norway (43%).

♦ In the UK, 54% of fans said they would support regulations to improve opportunities for ethnic/racial minority candidates applying for jobs at football clubs (which comes following similar legislation being brought

in by the FA). This figure is 64% in the US, where what is known as the 'Rooney Rule' has been implemented along these lines.

♦ In Germany and Switzerland, following controversies this summer relating to abuse aimed at Mesut Ozil and players of Albanian heritage representing the Swiss national team, nearly a quarter of fans from both countries would feel uncomfortable with a player of different ethnic / racial background representing their national or club teams (77% comfort for both).

♦ Respondents from Ghana (83%), Colombia (77%), and Nigeria (75%) are most in favour of deducting points from teams whose fans commit racist abuse. Russian (34%), Ukrainian (42%), and Dutch (45%) fans are least in favour of such a policy.

♦ Fans in Brazil (61%), Portugal (60%), and France (44%) feel most confident they would know how to report incidents of racist abuse. Fans in the UAE (9%), Ukraine (12%), and Egypt (12%) feel least confident.

21 November 2018

Original source: Kick It Out - English football's equality and inclusion organisation
www.kickitout.org

Islamophobia is a form of racism – like antisemitism it's time it got its own definition

It has become so normalised in our society yet we struggle to define it. Our report will provide something we can all get behind.

By Anna Soubry and Wes Streeting

In recent years, British Muslim communities across the UK have experienced an increase in Islamophobia. To eradicate the deeprooted nature of Islamophobia from our society, each of us has a responsibility to tackle prejudice wherever it occurs.

But the absence of a clear understanding of Islamophobia has allowed it to become normalised within our society and even socially acceptable, able to pass what Baroness Warsi described as the "dinner table test". The consequences have been horrific.

The killing of grandfather Makram Ali outside a Finsbury Park mosque in 2017, the murder of another elderly Muslim male, Mushin Ahmed, in Rotherham in 2015 and the brutal stabbing of Mohammed Saleem in Birmingham in 2013, serve as grave reminders of the perils of what can happen when Islamophobia goes unchecked.

The attacks on hijab wearing women in the street, the bomb threats made to places of worship, through to the coining of "Punish a Muslim Day", has left vulnerable Britons feeling unsafe to go about their daily lives.

Islamophobic hate crime is a growing problem. Recent statistics highlight how attacks on Muslims have seen the highest increase.

Nevertheless hate crime is the just the tip of the iceberg in terms of the underlying causes which remain hidden from sight. While we can tackle the overt manifestations of Islamophobia in the form of hate crimes, we are less conscious and less clued up about tackling that which lies beneath the waterline.

Last year marked the 20th anniversary of the Runnymede Commission's first report, which brought Islamophobia into

the English lexicon. And 2019 will mark the 20th anniversary of the MacPherson Report. Between these two landmark events and in the backdrop to the growing phenomenon of Islamophobia, the All-Party Parliamentary Group on British Muslims, which we chair, initiated the inquiry into a working definition on Islamophobia as a catalyst for building a common understanding of the causes and consequences of Islamophobia. If we can define the problem, we stand a better chance of properly addressing it.

Our six-month-long inquiry heard from academics, lawyers, activists, victim groups and British Muslim organisations, as well as firsthand accounts from communities in Manchester, Sheffield, Birmingham and London. Today we publish our report, Islamophobia Defined, which provides a working definition of Islamophobia:

"Islamophobia is rooted in racism and is a type of racism that targets expressions of Muslimness or perceived Muslimness."

The definition is further exemplified by case study examples and real life incidents, presented within a framework resembling the International Holocaust Remembrance Alliance's definition of antisemitism, providing guidelines on how the definition can be applied.

This isn't about protecting a religion from criticism, but about protecting people from discrimination. The APPG on British Muslims received countless submissions detailing the racialised manner in which the Muslimness of an individual was used to attack Muslims or those perceived to be Muslims. The racialisation of Muslims proceeds on the basis of their racial and religious identity, or perceived identity, from white converts receiving racialised sobriquets such as "paki", Muslim women attacked due to their perceived dress, bearded men attacked for the personification of a Muslim identity or even turban wearing Sikhs attacked due to the perception of Muslimness.

The adoption of this definition provides an opportunity to help the nation turn the tide against this pernicious form of racism, enabling a better understanding to tackle both hate crimes and the underlying institutional prejudices preventing ordinary British Muslims from achieving their level best across different aspects of our society.

By and large British Muslims feel able to practise their religion freely in Britain, and most believe that Islam is compatible with the British way of life. In recent years, we have seen British Muslims make huge strides from the first Muslim home secretary and mayor of London, to the first female Muslim British Bake Off champion, through to the ordinary doctors, teachers, business leaders, police officers and the service men and women of our nation. These few examples demonstrate the huge potential for Muslims to flourish in Britain, but these few examples can't take away the huge barriers ordinary Muslims face to reach such positions.

We strongly encourage the government, political parties, statutory bodies, public and private institutions to adopt this definition in helping to achieve a fairer society for all, as we believe the conclusion to the inquiry will become the benchmark for defining and tackling the scourge of Islamophobia.

The mistakes of this past summer and the denial of political parties to accept a definition of antisemitism must now not be repeated with another minority community. We need to get to the point where it is as socially unacceptable to be Islamophobic as it is to be homophobic or sexist. The adoption of this definition does just that.

27 November 2018

How to call out racism without destroying your relationships

Though it seems painfully obvious to some, the definition of racism isn't so clear cut to others.

By Faima Bakar

Though it seems painfully obvious to some, the definition of racism isn't so clear cut to others.

The idea that racism is always overt, like calling someone the N-word or being physically or verbally abusive, is prevalent.

But many people of colour will argue it's more insidious and subtle than that.

Racism can manifest institutionally, through microaggressions, jokes, comments impinging on stereotypes, and even unwelcoming stares.

Though these experiences are not physically violent, they can leave lasting impressions on people of colour and make them feel like an outsider, that their sensibilities don't matter and that they are not important.

For those on the receiving end of these prejudices, it's difficult to call out especially where personal relationships are involved.

And where racism is called out in professional settings, it can have a detrimental effect on people's careers.

One survey by People Management found that 95% of ethnic minority respondents had experienced occasional or persistent microaggressions during their career, compared to 16% of white respondents.

The same study found that ethnic minorities are also less likely to progress in their career.

In social settings, calling out racism means uncomfortable feelings and may even result in losing a friend.

So how do you gently call someone out in a way that doesn't irreparably damage the relationship.

For 16-year-old Kiyara*, the insensitive comments from her step-dad make her uncomfortable.

He has made references to her Canadian Aboriginal ancestry in a derogatory way which has left her reeling.

She tells Metro.co.uk: 'My mum and I are Métis, but my step-dad insists on using words like "Indian, redskin" etc. I don't know why but my mum just stands by and doesn't do anything.

'He also perpetuates stereotypes all the time but it's more like thinly veiled racism. I've tried telling him that it's really rude but he just brushes me off.

'One time I even told him about a boy at school catcalling me and all he says are "well isn't it true you Indian women are easy? You probably gave him that idea."

'He insists he's not racist but he treats all POC differently than he does white people.

'The comments really hurt my feelings and just make me uncomfortable. I've tried explaining it to him quite a few times but he just brushes me off and calls it a "joke".'

Therapist and public speaker Marilyn Devonish says anyone hoping to call out racist behaviour may receive a similar, defensive response.

One of the most common responses her clients reference when unpacking an experience of confronting racism is: 'Why now? I've been doing and saying this for years, and you've said nothing before!'

Letting things go in the past may have worked but Marilyn says it doesn't mean it needs to continue.

She tells Metro.co.uk: 'Previously they have "let it go", "sucked it up", "not made a big deal about it", and/or, depending upon your exposure and background, endured the sting of the often constant microaggressions.

'But it's not that everyone has suddenly woken up to racism or is looking for things, more that it has gotten to the point where enough is enough.

'It can be a challenging issue because race speaks to the core of who we are as human beings, and can feel like an attack on our character or heritage. Sometimes things are said in the heat of the moment, particularly where you cannot have that conversation again.

'Those are the times where a decision has to be made about whether to walk away, or address the situation.

'I always suggest taking a breath and possibly counting to ten to give yourself a chance to decide how best to proceed. Taking a deep breath clears your head.

'Then ask yourself what you would like to achieve? Is it to raise a specific incident, open up a wider conversation, get an apology, clear the air, be heard, highlight and signpost, etc?.

'I would encourage parties on all sides to be open to listening.

'If you're white, be prepared to hear those of colour speak with some level of passion and emotion, and do your best not to take everything personally and retreat into a defensive huff.

'Also avoid "Blacksplaining", which is telling a black person how they should feel, what something means, or explaining away their experience.'

Even for white people trying to explain to other white people the implications of their speech and action, it can be difficult.

Jasper, 19, also has struggled to make his family see that certain behaviours are not acceptable but has been subject to ridicule or alienation.

He tells Metro.co.uk: 'I wrote a letter to my mother that tried to explain the situation as best as I could, and asked that she do some research using the resources I provided before trying to defend herself.

'Her immediate response was to send the letter to the rest of the family, and then come confront me about how not racist she is. I asked her if she had looked at anything I sent, to which she hadn't.

'She still didn't understand how it was possible she was racist since she "loves Black people." Any information she read had just gone in one ear and out the other, but I attempted to explain that racism extends past the extremists, but she kept avoiding the topic and saying "Well you're entitled to your opinion."'

Jasper eventually gave up but planned to keep trying with the rest of the family, however, that also didn't work.

He added: 'Since her initial response was to tell the entire family that I hated them, I had to deal with everyone at once instead of one at a time.

'I already deal with a lot of anxiety, so my entire family thinking I randomly decided I don't like them anymore certainly didn't make me feel any better. Any attempts I made after all of this is just met with the excuse that I'm spending too much time talking to "people on the internet" and I've been brainwashed into some extremist ideology and nothing I say has any merit.

'So at this point I've pretty much stopped trying to change their perspective, and just hope that they decide to educate themselves one day.'

Cases like Kiyara and Jasper's aren't unique. Many people have been hurt by comments from their family members, friends, colleagues, and strangers.

And being expected to explain problematic behaviours also takes a toll on people.

Anti-racism campaigner and author of The Good Ally, Nova Reid, says ultimately your own peace of mind is most important.

She tells Metro.co.uk: 'Decide if the relationship is worth it. You do not have to be a martyr and challenge every instance of racism, especially if you are Black or a person of colour.

'You may receive further racism, be gaslit, or be shut down and ignored by doing so. If you decide to engage think about if you want to give feedback at the moment, in private, or retrospectively on another day.'

Nova also has advice for white people who want to be an ally and call out racism themselves instead of relying on people of colour to do the job.

She adds: 'If you're white and giving feedback on another white person's racism – share resources and invite them in to learn more. Say things like: "I often get it wrong too, but that's part of the process – if you want to read more about it I found this really helpful check out XXX".'

Therapist Hendrix Hammond also has similar advice which encourages people being told they're being racist to be introspective and calm.

He tells us: 'The means in which you engage people around a sensitive conversation like racism should always be from a place of non-judgment, curiosity and willingness to listen.

'That is the first step to creating the space to have difficult conversations which can transform beliefs, behaviours and relationships.'

*Name has been changed.

28 September 2020

Tackling racism is about more than curriculum

Education is key to tackling racism, says Jeffery Quaye. But what obstacles have school leaders and teachers had to overcome when it comes to race and what does the future hold?

By Dr Jeffrey Quaye

Education is key to tackling racism, says Jeffery Quaye. But what obstacles have school leaders and teachers had to overcome when it comes to race and what does the future hold?

The senseless and horrific killing of George Floyd in Minneapolis has ignited a global discussion about racism and the need for change. It has also brought into sharp focus the traumatic prejudice I and other black people in this country have experienced.

The killing and protests dominate the political arena. Boris Johnson has said that "racism and racist violence have no place in our society". But it should not take an unlawful public execution to stun the consciousness of the British people.

Sajid Javid, the former chancellor, has called for the government to set "a new ambition for breaking down" racial barriers. Meanwhile, Matt Hancock, the health secretary, has been forced to defend the diversity of the government after critics pointed out that there are no black members of the Cabinet. He also claimed the UK is not a racist country, yet black people in British society continue to experience racism.

As a black teacher and leader in education, I see the transformational power of education to eradicate racism in our society. Huge strides have been made over the past two decades to tackle institutional and structural racism within education and to promote diversity and inclusion. Schools have championed this work with a focus on educating pupils about multicultural Britain. The introduction of British values has raised the expectations for mutual respect and schools are tackling racism when it manifests in pupil behaviour.

> *'I felt pressure to work ten times harder to be recognised'.*

However, there are still disparities in the experience of black teachers that we need to have honest conversations about. I have faced obstacles because of my race since I started teaching in 2003. At Aspirations Academies Trust, race is not a barrier to development and career progression, but elsewhere others appear to have wanted to make teaching difficult for me. From being given incredibly challenging classes to lack of leadership support, my awareness of the covert racism people of BAME background face in schools has been sharpened over the years.

As a classroom teacher I encountered many situations in which white colleagues were not performing at the required standards, but schools leaders did not raise any concerns. However, the expectations set for my work remained high, even when the conditions did not enable me to reach such goals. I experienced a deafening silence among white colleagues when black staff were treated unfairly by their leaders.

I found my leadership role in one school to be lonely – and one where I felt pressure to work ten times harder to be recognised. We still have a disproportionately low number of school leaders from a BAME background because education does not always actively encourage and promote black leaders into senior management. Consequently, the senior leadership can be entirely white in a school that serves predominantly black pupils.

The dominant worldview is that black leaders are not up to the role of leadership or not of equal value as their white colleagues. This can create spaces where minority ethnic teachers feel uncomfortable in their job.

While we are inspiring the next generation and raising the aspirations of all pupils, black teachers and education leaders experience an institutional racism that manifests in many subtle forms, such as schools not providing the same level of recognition or opportunities to black teachers and negative perceptions of black colleagues going unchallenged. To tackle that structural racism, teachers need to be educated about unconscious bias, and internalised negative views of black people need to be challenged with an alternative worldview.

It can be done. The working model Aspirations uses gives black teachers equal value through a collegial working environment. Steve and Paula Kenning, the trust's chief executives, ensure all teachers and staff are made to feel equal and valued and black staff have good representation in decision-making processes.

Education should be an equaliser of all men and women, regardless of race. But eradicating racism can't simply be the work of curriculum. It is about changing our practices too.

13 June 2020

A brief history of black and Asian history in England

Racism and resistance

Imperial European powers found ways to justify the barbaric slave system and the invasion, colonisation and expropriation of foreign lands for the expansion of their wealth.

Britain amongst them created a hierarchy with white Europeans at the top and Africans and Asians at the bottom. Racism became embedded into the nation's structures of power, culture, education and identity.

People from Africa, the Caribbean and Asia were encouraged by government to come to England. But on arrival here they often faced racism and discrimination, which was not illegal in Britain until 1965.

Racist attacks

In 1919, there were large-scale racist attacks on 'coloured' communities in London, Manchester, Liverpool, Hull, South Shields as well as parts of Scotland and Wales.

There were other large-scale attacks in Liverpool in 1948, in Nottingham and Notting Hill in 1958 and at other times and places throughout the century since 1918.

One of the most well-known racist murders is that of teenager Stephen Lawrence in 1993. There have been many murders in the past, including, Akhtar Ali Baig in East Ham in 1980. Kelso Cochrane was also murdered in Notting Hill in 1959 and Charles Wootton, in Liverpool in 1919.

Racist practices, policies and politics

Although migrant workers have been vital for the growth of Britain's economy and public services, racism has sometimes been widespread. There was the 'colour bar' that prevented 'coloured' people obtaining jobs and accommodation, fighting for British boxing titles or even joining the armed services or serving as officers in them. Some laws were openly racist too, such as the 1925 Coloured Alien Seamen's Order or the 1981 British Nationality Act.

There have been openly racist speeches by leading politicians too. Seeking to create divisions and stir up racism Enoch Powell's infamous 'Rivers of Blood' tirade in 1968 is a well-known example. And then there are the activities of politically racist organisations such as the National Front.

Resistance, protest and defence

In response those of African, Caribbean and Asian descent have been forced to find various forms of resistance alongside allies. They organised political actions or demonstrations such as the Grunwick Strike in 1976 and the Black People's Day of Action in 1981 in London. There were various protests against police and racist violence in the 1970s and 1980s.

Sometimes it meant forming defence organisations such as the League of Coloured Peoples and the first Indian Workers' Association established in the 1930s, or the Black People's Alliance in the 1970s.

At other times, communities responded by establishing places of refuge and sanctuary. There was the widespread supplementary school movement often favoured in Caribbean communities. There were also centres such as Africa House in Camden in the 1930s, or cultural centres, such as the Drum in Birmingham in the 1990s.

Another England

Black and Asian histories are a vital part of England's story. Yet in our books, at our historic sites and in our records they're not well represented.

The above information is reprinted with kind permission from Historic England.
© 2020 Historic England.

www.historicengland.org.uk

How HR, D&I practitioners, CEOs & line managers can support black colleagues

By Petunia Thomas, MBA CPCC

Black colleagues and network groups have been dealing with, at a conscious and subconscious level: their own experiences of racism past and present, the external atrocity of George Floyd's murder and countless others, the impact of the mainstream media narrative around the disproportionate number of `BAME` covid deaths, as well as trying to `show up` and continue to be professional for work.

'Organisations cannot underestimate the unspoken exhaustion, emotional drain, burden and trauma black colleagues have been experiencing during this period – overlaid with the covid challenges - even though they may still be turning up to work and being 'physically' present via Zoom/Teams/Skype/GoTo/Hangout etc.' It's great that a number of companies have been openly inviting feedback and listening to personal experiences and opinions of their black colleagues at this time. However a word of caution: to be repeatedly and continuously relied upon for voluntary sharing to help educate/lead on teaching for senior leaders and colleagues, on top of their actual day job which they were hired for, must be met with empathy and sensitivity to their wellbeing.

'It is important not to place any new burden of responsibility on internal black colleagues but it is paramount for them to receive the emotional support they require right now.'

There are mental, emotional health and wellbeing factors to consider – particularly for black colleagues who, have stepped forward and been willing to share their experiences of racism and micro-aggressions at work with colleagues, panels, teams and the organisation. Non-black HR, leaders and D&I practitioners and line managers need to support them as they do - through 1:1 conversations, and employee assistance programmes (EAPs) which have black counsellors. Plus, there are self-care tips for black people experiencing trauma during this period.

'Additionally, it is important to recognise that, just as for other corporate strategic initiatives or operational plans where black staff are not specifically singled out to deliver or prepare unless it is already part of their role in those particular departments, it is also not, in the case of black lives, the role of black colleagues and networks to suddenly be singled out and additionally pressurised into drafting corporate race action plans on behalf of their organisations over and above their current work (find out more about the `cultural tax` or `black tax`). Such work continues to be the responsibility of the leadership who are accountable for delivering these plans, albeit they may receive input and suggestions via listening groups for black colleagues, which inform their corporate recommendations and strategic plans.

Leaders can draw in black, external expertise if there is no explicit role in the organisation that already specifically and formally covers this activity.'

Remember, black colleagues in the main just want to be able to work in an environment that feels psychologically safe for them to be authentic and where they feel they can belong. This safety enables and empowers them to share – whether it be via informal chats, conversations, talks, emails, focus/listening groups etc, so the more supportive, open and understanding the environment is for them, the better.

By all means, have the conversation about race but also be prepared to allocate and invest resources to engage external black professionals and black-led businesses to expertly facilitate the internal dialogue. This will also, importantly, relieve the stress and strain also on black HR &D&I professionals and networks, who should not be viewed as the sole corporate solution or new source and fount of knowledge for `all things black`.

They are overwhelmed at this time and they too need support so they can breathe.

Seven things you can do to support black colleagues over the next six to twelve months:

1. ACKNOWLEDGE & ASK:

Simply acknowledging and explicitly stating the awfulness of the George Floyd atrocity, showing compassion by asking how they are but saying that you know they may not want to talk about it, is a good place to start.

Offering a listening ear if they want to talk and listen to understand rather than counter-argue or engage in debate or discussion. Ask if they mind you asking a question, if you have something you'd like to understand from the experience they shared. This is not about general fact-finding but about making that personal connection through compassion and empathy from hearing their story. Be aware that some may want to share but others may not be willing or able to at this time. Think about how you do support those colleagues who do share, as well as those who can't.

And beware of repeatedly calling on them over time to relive their experiences or relying on them as a `shortcut` to personal learning about racial inequality past and present.

2. LISTEN TO UNDERSTAND:

Be prepared to be led by black colleagues and networks on how you engage them to understand their stories, to better understand their lived experiences.

Secondly, revisit career conversations held with black colleagues to date. What have individuals shared as future roles, support required, training and development opportunities etc which may have hitherto been overlooked by your organisation? Do you understand their current aspirations? Can you see the full range of their skills and talents and potential beyond the current role they are doing? What should you be doing from now to retain and develop each colleague in a way that could help address the disproportionate under-representation gap at senior levels? Line managers and HR together can collect this data.

3. ENGAGE & INVEST:

Conversations should encompass asking black colleagues what the company can do to support them individually, not just what they can do individually or as a network to help the company at this stage. [The networks have often been built upon in an uncompensated capacity, with little or no budget by those who want to do well in their day job and who have given additional personal time, energy, passion and sometimes personal sacrifice. This foundation may need to be reviewed, such that hitherto voluntary time given is valued and explicitly acknowledged in some formal way, with appropriate budget, level of investment and formal recognition through internal systems to deliver added value to the organisation and its members.

Please feel free to make use of the waste paper bin.

4. SELF-EDUCATE TO RAISE PERSONAL AWARENESS:

This is an important period for non-black CEOs and leaders, HR, line managers to separately take the time to invest in self-education. There are plenty of resources that have been made available, so beginning a course of study and learning, downloading some of the multiple resources and book lists and working your way through them would be time well spent. Delving into a recommended book or film may be a good start. It is a willingness go beyond rhetoric, external media or a moment to internalise personal learnings that will make the difference.

5. REFLECT MORE DEEPLY:

Intentional reflection on systemic and structural systems and barriers that have existed for black people, no matter how uncomfortable it may feel at times, is also key. This critical phase for personal reflection should not be overlooked, minimised, ignored or dismissed in place of a corporate response or stance on racial inequality. A personal commitment is also required. Perhaps create a separate journal to capture personal insights and adding to it over the coming days, months and years will help you chart your learning. It is the beginning of a journey, and is the necessary groundwork to authentically come alongside your black colleagues.

6. AMPLIFY LEARNING & SHARING – A TWO-WAY PROCESS:

Now presents the opportunity for non-black line managers, leaders, HR & D&I practitioners, to individually and intentionally reflect on what that means in terms of personal values and potential behaviour change to achieve racial equality. This is key in demonstrating the important qualities of compassion and empathy in active anti-racist allyship. For those embarking on this journey for the first time or more deeply, be prepared to also openly share your insights back with your black colleagues. Demonstration of

your personal and ongoing reflection, learning and action will be important in establishing your own credibility and perceived authenticity in the face of your black colleagues and in your organisation.

7. APPLY THE LEARNINGS & TAKE ACTION:

Diligently and swiftly begin to apply the feedback, findings and recommendations to plan, invest and follow through with committed, coherent, corporate actions across the employee lifecycle and in recruitment. Revisit the McGregor-Smith Review, and establish the organisational infrastructure to implement the actions.

This will involve engaging external black professionals and black-led, black-founded and black-owned businesses to partner with over the coming months and years, particularly for organisations that specifically made public commitments and pledges around black lives. And it will, through external public accountability, measurement and reporting, demonstrate genuine alliance, as well as create the uplift to positively impact broader social and economic justice and inclusion.

As we intentionally create and maintain empowering environments for black colleagues to share, develop and progress - and keep them safe and support them in doing so - we are making room for their talent and potential to also thrive and flourish in diverse workplaces. And, all together we are establishing more actively inclusive cultures for all through transformational systemic and behaviour change, for organisational, individual and societal growth and success for now - for generations to come and for good.

1 July 2020

Racism isn't just a US problem; to fight it in the UK we need to change how it's taught in schools

It's time to move away from a 'whitewashed' curriculum, where black history is omitted or taught only in terms of colonialism and slavery.

By Rachel Cranshaw

The first time she was taught African history as anything other than a sidebar to European adventures, Lavinya Stennett was at university. Reflecting on how little she and her fellow students had been taught about black history at school – usually short references to the American civil rights leader Martin Luther King or the South African anti-apartheid leader Nelson Mandela – inspired her last year to set up The Black Curriculum, a campaign for black British history to be embedded into the UK curriculum rather than limited to Black History Month (if that). The proposal includes four modules: art history; migration; politics and the legal system; and land and the environment.

"[University] was the first time I had studied African history that incorporated a non-Eurocentric perspective," she told me, speaking at the end of a long day in a week that has seen her campaign propelled into the spotlight as Britain reacted to the killing of George Floyd in the US by a police officer. "The school curriculum is very whitewashed, and black history is usually either omitted entirely, or taught only in terms of colonialism and slavery, rather than black people's achievements."

Social media is currently awash with demands (including a petition to the Secretary of State for Education, Gavin Williamson) for children to be taught about the reality of Britain's racist, colonial past (exported, of course, to the US), and while Stennett agrees this is absolutely necessary, she stresses the importance of achieving "an equal balance between confronting the hard parts of black British history and [...] celebrating role models and the contributions black people have made to our society".

Learning beyond slavery and colonialism

Stennett's mother used to buy books on black inventors as part of ensuring a more comprehensive education, but not all black children – and very few white children, though of course this is the best place for families to start – may receive this independent investment.

And this is not the only major omission on the curriculum. The Black Lives Matter movement has woken many (white) people up to the sentiment of a much-cited Angela Davis observation: that "In a racist society it is not enough to be non-racist, we must be anti-racist."

What it means to be anti-racist

The multicultural junior school I attended in the Nineties took a proactive approach to teaching pupils about racism – but my formal education did not make me aware of my own white privilege. It did not hold me accountable. It taught me, to borrow words from a 2014 blog post by US author and poet Scott Woods, that racism amounted to "conscious hate, when [it] is bigger than that. Racism is a complex system of social and political levers and pulleys set up generations ago to continue working on the behalf of whites at other people's expense, whether whites know/like it or not. Racism is so insidious it doesn't care if you are a white person who likes black people; it's still going to find a way to infect how you deal with people who don't look like you. There is no anti-racist certification class. It's a set of socioeconomic traps and cultural values that are fired up every time we interact with the world."

Stennett, now age 23, started school eight years after me, and agreed: "The teaching of racism individualises it and removes the structure. It's very polarised, with no understanding of the complexity; of things like microaggressions and tokenism."

I spoke to Ged Grebby, Chief Executive of Show Racism the Red Card, which works with schools to teach anti-racism, utilising the status of footballers and other high-profile individuals. The charity was established in 1996, and I remember it from my own youth. He confirms that "things haven't moved on" since then – anti-racism and black British history are still not part of the curriculum (though the charity does help train every teacher in Wales).

This is against a backdrop of a rise in race hate crime: there has been an 11 per cent increase in England and Wales from 2018-19 alone. Black people are twice as likely to die in police custody in Britain. People from a Black and Minority Ethnic (BAME) background are up to twice as likely to die from Covid-19, the government's report on which Grebby described as "appalling", with no conclusions.

Grebby told me the teaching of "Citizenship", which includes lessons on politics, parliament and voting as well as human rights, justice, the law and the economy, offered some hope when it was made mandatory in 2001, but has ultimately failed to deliver as it is too vague. Asked what he thinks is the most important change we need in schools right now, Grebby said: "Anti-racism on the curriculum, and more time for teachers to teach it."

What could the curriculum look like?

Primary school teachers tell me Black History Month in October may be consigned to a single assembly, if acknowledged at all. At secondary school the picture is just as troubling. One teacher I spoke to, Sophie Thomas, explained that in the south London school where she works, and where the majority of students come from a black African or Caribbean background, Black History Month is never acknowledged, and the lack of black faces extends beyond History and Personal, Social and Health Education (PSHE) into subjects such as English.

Changes made by Michael Gove in 2014 to the GCSE syllabus mean there is now a predominant focus on 19th-century

literature and Shakespeare, with the modern texts available to choose from "pretty pale, male and stale, and then some tokenistic poetry written by black and brown people, and some women". In many schools, this limited syllabus begins in Year 7 because of a desire to demonstrate a clear trajectory to Ofsted.

"Teachers are not trained or empowered to teach certain topics through an anti-racist lens – and school leaders do not understand this," Thomas adds. Another petition doing the rounds currently calls for these texts to be updated with seminal contemporary works such as Why I'm no Longer Talking to White People about Race, by Reni Eddo-Lodge – but she suggests, chiming with Stennett's approach, that even better outcomes are possible.

"I am mixed race black Caribbean and white, and I have [tried] as an English teacher to compile a reading list where black and brown writers are featured and it's not constant stories of tragedy and oppression. It is important to teach those stories, but what is even more important is stories of success. Black kids don't want to hear about a history of oppression every time a black person is mentioned in their lessons."

Now is the moment to change

Everyone I spoke to agreed the potential for real change at the moment was unprecedented. Grebby described the momentum as "incredible", while Stennett said: "I have not seen people mobilise like this in my lifetime. Everyone is shocked and outraged.

"It has to turn into something," she concluded. "There is no better time to create a better society."

5 June 2020

Key Facts

- The Equality Act 2010 says you must not be discriminated against because of your race. (page 3)

- According to a YouGov survey, virtually identical numbers of people believe racism exists in the country today (84%) as believe it existed 30 years ago (86%). (page 4)

- When asked about the Metropolitan police today, one in two (50%) think it is institutionally racist; seven in ten Black Britons (69%) share this view compared to around half of other BAME groups. (page 6)

- Over half (56%) support the removal of all statues linked to slavery from British towns and cities; just 19% oppose this. (page 6)

- As a result of the Black Lives Matter protests this year, half of 18 to 24 year olds (49%) and Black people (48%) say they are listening to and reading more about issues related to racism now than before. (page 7)

- 'Reverse racism' is the concept that the dominant racial group in a society – white people – can experience racism at the hands of minority groups. (page 12)

- The word 'antisemitism' first appeared in the 19th century, when classification of people into different races was considered normal. (page 12)

- "Systemic racism", or "institutional racism", refers to how ideas of white superiority are captured in everyday thinking at a systems level: taking in the big picture of how society operates, rather than looking at one-on-one interactions. (page 15)

- In a Harvard study, only 10% of black candidates got interview offers when their race could be implied by their resume, but 25% got offers when their resumes were whitened. (page 16)

- In Australia, Indigenous people make up 2% of the Australian population, but 28% of the adult prison population. (page16)

- The number of minority ethnic students at top universities rose from 9% in 1995 to 18% in 2017. But gulfs remain. In 2016-17, 3.6% of black Caribbean A-level students got three top grades or better compared with 11.2% of whites. Only one black British student was admitted to Corpus Christi College, Oxford in 2015, 2016 and 2017 collectively. (page 17)

- An investigation by The Independent revealed that the number of racist incidents in universities across the UK surged by more than 60 per cent between 2015 and 2017. (page 25)

- Globally, over half of football fans (54%) have witnessed racist abuse while watching a football game. Only 28% would know how to appropriately report such racist incidents. (page 29)

- Globally, 74% of fans want FIFA to consider previous racist abuse when awarding countries international tournaments. The hosts of the 2026 World Cup are in agreement, with 77% of Americans wanting this, 76% of Mexicans, and 77% of Canadians. (page 29)

- Fans in Norway (95%), Sweden (94%), and Brazil (93%) feel most comfortable with a player of different ethnic / racial background representing their national or club team. Fans in Saudi Arabia (11%), Lebanon (15%), and the UAE (19%) feel least comfortable. (page 29)

- One survey by People Management found that 95% of ethnic minority respondents had experienced occasional or persistent microaggressions during their career, compared to 16% of white respondents. (page 32)

- There has been an 11 per cent increase in race hate crime in England and Wales from 2018-19. (page 39)

- Black people are twice as likely to die in police custody in Britain. (page 39)

Antisemitism

Antisemitism is hostility to, or prejudice or discrimination against Jews as a religious, ethnic or racial group.

BAME

An acronym which stands for Black, Asian and Minority Ethnic backgrounds.

Discrimination

Unfair treatment of someone because of the group/class they belong to.

Ethnic minority

A group of people who are different in their ancestry, culture and traditions from the majority of the population.

Gypsy, Roma and Travellers

Groups of people who traditionally pursue a nomadic lifestyle which involves moving around from place to place. English gypsies and Irish travellers are protected under the Race Relations Act. This is because they are members of a community with a shared history stretching back over hundreds of years and are recognised by as law as a distinct ethnic minority group.

Harrassment

Usually persistent (but not always), a behaviour that is intended to cause distress and offence. It can occur on the school playground, in the workplace or at home.

Hate crime

This term can be used to describe criminal behaviour where the perpetrator is motivated by hostility or demonstrates hostility towards an aspect or 'protected characteristic' of their victim's identity, such as race or religion.

Islamophobia

An extreme fear and hatred of Islam and people who follow the Islam faith, otherwise known as Muslims.

Multiculturalism

A number of different cultures coexisting side by side, for example within a school or a country.

Racial discrimination

Racial discrimination occurs when a person is treated less favourably because of their colour, race, nationality or ethnic or national origins.

Racial prejudice

The belief and prejudgement that one race is inferior to another. Feeling hatred towards another race just because they are different.

Racism

The belief and prejudgement that one race is superior to another/behaving in a negative or harmful way to someone because of their race.

Reverse racism/discrimination

A perceived discrimination or prejudice against the dominant or majority group in society.

Systemic racism

Also known as 'institutional racism'. This term refers to racism that is built into the structure of society and different institutions (e.g.schools, police, government).

The Race Relations Act 1976

The Race Relations Act 1976 is concerned with people's actions and the effects of their actions, not their opinions or beliefs. The Act makes it illegal to racially discriminate against anyone. It also aims to promote racial equality and good race relations.

Xenophobia

A fear of or hostility to foreigners, people from different cultures or strangers.

Activities

Brainstorming

♦ In small groups, discuss what you know about racism.

♦ What is the difference between racism and ethnic discrimination?

♦ What is meant by 'systemic' or institutional racism?

♦ What is the Black Lives Matter movement about?

Research

♦ Conduct an anonymous questionnaire amongst your friends, family and peers to find out whether they think racism and religious hatred have increased in recent years. Your questionnaire should include at least five different questions. What examples of racism can they give from what they've witnessed in real life, or what they've seen in the news or on social media. When you have gathered your results, create a short presentation of your findings to share with your class. Include tables and graphs if you can.

♦ In small groups, look online for news stories reporting examples of systemic racism in the following institutions:

· UK politics

· Education

· The police

· Football

How many stories or examples did you find? Share and compare with the rest of your class.

Design

♦ Choose one of the articles from this book and create an illustration that highlights the key themes of the piece.

♦ Imagine you work for an anti-racist charity or campaign group. Design a poster that could be displayed in public places such as bus stops or shopping arcades that will highlight your cause.

♦ Imagine you are attending an anti-racism protest. Design an eye-catching placard with a slogan to take with you.

♦ In small groups, design a storyboard for a series of YouTube videos highlighting everyday microaggressions experienced by different racial groups and ethnic minorities. You can use the article by Dina Asher-Smith: *Think racism hasn't affected me? It's there almost every day* on page 13; and the article *Microaggressions are not a harmless form of racism – they have a huge impact* on page 20 for reference.

Oral

♦ Read the article on page 9 *The philosophical flaw in saying "All Lives Matter"* Of course, all lives do matter, but why does the author of this piece think it is a flawed response in the context of the Black Lives Matter movement? Discuss as a class.

♦ A lot of high profile sports people and celebrities have 'taken the knee' as a gesture of support for the Black Lives Matter movement. Divide the class into those in favour and those against to debate the motion: 'Athletes and famous people should not engage in political protest.'

♦ Look at the graph on page 6 showing the extent to which BAME Britons support the Black Lives Matter movement. In small groups, discuss why you think some groups support it more than others.

Reading/writing

♦ Write a definition of the term 'white privilege' and compare it with a classmate's.

♦ Imagine you are a an Agony Aunt/Uncle and you have received a letter from a young child asking you 'Why are some people racist?' Write an email/letter in response.

♦ Compose a selection of anti-racist social media posts for Twitter, Facebook, and Instagram. The posts should act as a series of hard-hitting messages which call out everyday racism UK. You may also include links to external websites, videos and photos which provide further information if you think this is helpful.

♦ Select one of the following phrases and write a short poem or piece of prose expressing its meaning to you:

· Silence is violence

· I can't breathe

· Black lives matter

Acknowledgements

The publisher is grateful for permission to reproduce the material in this book. While every care has been taken to trace and acknowledge copyright, the publisher tenders its apology for any accidental infringement or where copyright has proved untraceable. The publisher would be pleased to come to a suitable arrangement in any such case with the rightful owner.

The material reproduced in *ISSUES* books is provided as an educational resource only. The views, opinions and information contained within reprinted material in *ISSUES* books do not necessarily represent those of Independence Educational Publishers and its employees.

Images

Cover image and image on page 17 courtesy of iStock. All other images courtesy of Pixabay and Unsplash, except page 1: Shutterstock.

Illustrations

Simon Kneebone: pages 3, 27 & 35. Angelo Madrid: pages 9, 32 & 37.

Additional acknowledgements

With thanks to the Independence team: Shelley Baldry, Danielle Lobban, Jackie Staines and Jan Sunderland.

Tracy Biram

Cambridge, September 2020